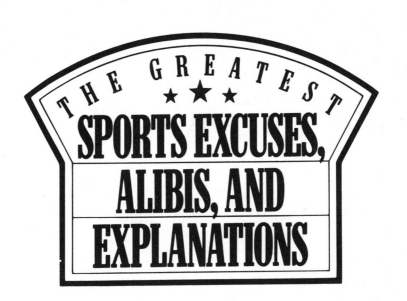

THE GREATEST
★ ★ ★
SPORTS EXCUSES, ALIBIS, AND EXPLANATIONS

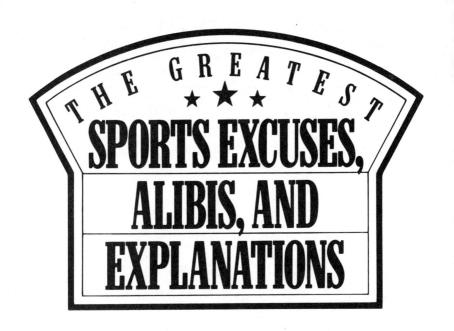

THE GREATEST
★ ★ ★
SPORTS EXCUSES, ALIBIS, AND EXPLANATIONS

JEFF PARIETTI

CB

CONTEMPORARY
BOOKS

CHICAGO

Library of Congress Cataloging-in-Publication Data

Parietti, Jeff.
     The greatest sports excuses, alibis, and explanations /
Jeff Parietti.
          p.   cm.
     ISBN 0-8092-4088-2
     1. Sports—Quotations, maxims, etc.   2. Sports—
Humor.   I. Title.
GV707.P34   1990
796'.0207—dc20
                                                              90-35028
                                                              CIP

Cover and interior illustrations by Dave Krainik.

Published by Contemporary Books, Inc.
180 North Michigan Avenue, Chicago, Illinois 60601
Manufactured in the United States of America
International Standard Book Number: 0-8092-4088-2

Contents

Introduction

Think back to the last time you had to come up with a quick excuse or explanation for something that happened or didn't happen. Maybe you were late for a business appointment or for a class. Perhaps you promised to run an important errand for a friend or your spouse and neglected to do it. Or maybe you bobbled the ball and cost your team a victory in the local softball league.

Remember what it was like when someone put you on the spot for an explanation?

Now think of the athletes, coaches, and other figures associated with the world of sports. Think of their stress when inquiring minds ask why they surrendered that game-winning home run, dropped that "sure" touchdown pass in the end zone, or chose a particular strategy that backfired.

Well, what happens is that they become good at coming up with excuses and explanations to get themselves off the hook.

This compilation of excuses, alibis, and explanations includes quotes ranging from the big-name sports figures of the past and the present to the unknown Little Leaguer. To preserve the flavor of each quote, I have listed the team affiliation of those making the excuses at the time the excuses were made.

You will discover that those in the sporting world are

very creative in coming up with amusing, humorous, offbeat, and sometimes philosophical excuses and explanations for both their own and others' behavior.

They may find it convenient to blame their mistakes on ill fortune. Or as Notre Dame football coach Lou Holtz says:

"The man who complains about the way the ball bounces is likely the one who dropped it."

Of course, when things go wrong it is also human nature to blame others. As offensive lineman Blaine Nye once noted during his days with the Dallas Cowboys:

"It's not whether you win or lose but who gets the blame."

And a bumper sticker hanging in the New York Mets clubhouse during the 1988 season simply reinforces this fact of life:

"To err is human. To blame it on someone else is more human."

And if bad luck or teammates are not available as excuses, there is always the stadium or field of play. The old baseball standby excuse, "I lost it in the sun," was updated to "I lost it in the roof" when the first domed stadium, the Houston Astrodome, opened in 1964. It proved true Cleveland Indians president Gabe Paul's prediction about the Astrodome:

"It will revolutionize baseball; it will open a new area of alibis for the players."

And if cursing bad luck, teammates, or the stadium doesn't quite work, then there are always the ever-present, convenient targets of abuse—the officials.

As former National League umpire Beans Reardon once said, when asked if he thought some sort of high-.tech device might replace umpires in the future:

"It will never happen, because when you do that you've taken away all the alibis. Who can the managers blame losses on? Who can the pitchers and hitters blame their troubles on? Believe me, the umpire will always be with us."

Likewise, so will the excuses, alibis, and explanations.

1
From Here
to Eternity

FROM AGE TO AGE

To be a great excuse maker, you need to know that your age can always come in handy. In other words, claims of being too young can serve as an excuse just as well as claims of being too old. Of course, traveling the path from too young to too old also offers plenty of opportunities for producing ageless excuses.

... ...

Frank Mooney, manager of a Kings Beach, California, Little League team of seven- and eight-year-old boys, offering an excuse for a 27–9 loss in their opener:

"We've got a young team out there."

...

Tennis star Jimmy Connors, on the reason he decided not to buy a 1960 Rolls-Royce that he liked:

"When I got behind the wheel, I looked like a boy chauffeur."

...

3

Princeton basketball coach Pete Carril, on why he always seems so pessimistic:

> *"Probably because I didn't have enough toys when I was a kid."*

...

University of Minnesota football coach Cal Stoll, explaining his philosophy on playing freshmen:

> *"The best time to play a freshman is when he is a junior."*

...

Notre Dame football coach Lou Holtz, on why the Fighting Irish's 1988 opener against Michigan was to be played at night:

> *"It gives us longer to mature."*

...

Bill Yeoman, Houston Cougars football coach, after his young team lost seven of eight games:

> *"Young teams usually get better with age, but right now, the coaches are aging faster than the players."*

...

Guard Sam Worthen, 23, on why the Chicago Bulls waived him:

> *"I think they want to go with a younger group."*

...

Pitcher Jim McGlothlin, 30, on the reason the Chicago White Sox placed him on waivers:

"When you're 21, you're a prospect. When you're 30, you're a suspect."

...

New York Jets quarterback Joe Namath, on why turning 30 didn't bother him:

"I stopped counting once I was old enough to go into a bar, get a drink, and not get thrown out."

...

Jimmy Connors, 35, explaining experience:

"The problem is that when you get it, you're too damned old to do anything about it."

...

San Diego Chargers coach Sid Gillman on the best way to settle down young offensive linemen who jump offsides:

"Play your veterans."

...

When a ball fell between Cincinnati Reds left fielder Pete Rose, 43, and shortstop Angel Salazar, 23, during a game in Montreal, an anonymous press-box observer offered two possible explanations:

"I don't know if that was a communication gap or a generation gap."

...

When Johan Kriek, 31, defeated 17-year-old Michael Chang he was asked if the two had met before. Said Kriek:

"We played once before in the juniors. I was in the under-18s and he was in the under-2s."

...

The Philadelphia Phillies' Pete Rose, asked why he didn't behave like a 40-year-old:

"I'm 41."

...

Houston Astros manager Preston Gomez, explaining the effects of aging on intelligence:

"The older you get in baseball the smarter you get. The trouble with some players is that by the time they get smart their career is over."

...

St. Louis Cardinals pitcher Jim Kaat, 42, on what convinced him to return to play a 23rd major-league season despite his age:

"They offered me a contract and they're paying me."

...

Ancient Oakland Raiders placekicker George Blanda, 46, on why he didn't plan to coach when his playing career ended:

"I'm too old to coach."

...

Sam Snead, 77, on why he declined to play on the Professional Golfers' Association (PGA) Senior Tour:

"It's a grind trying to beat 60-year-old kids out there."

...

Ruth Rothfarb, 86, on why it would be tough to beat her best marathon time set six years earlier:

"You lose an awful lot of speed between 80 and 86."

AS TIME GOES BY

Poor time! Its job is simply to march on. But then there is sports with its time-outs and gridiron clashes that take 30 minutes to end after the two-minute warning. Does anybody really know what time it is? Here are some excuses and explanations for how time impacts sports.

... ...

Dr. Jack Rose, Cal State–Long Beach track coach, on why he selected an unusually early 10:15 A.M. starting time for a triangular college track meet:

> *"So I can get my lawn cut in the afternoon."*

...

National Football League (NFL) commissioner Pete Rozelle, explaining when the Super Bowl would start:

> *"The Super Bowl is like a 300-pound gorilla. It starts any time it wants."*

...

Dallas Cowboys defensive tackle Larry Cole, on why he went scoreless in the 1970s before finally scoring a touchdown on a fumble recovery in 1980:

> *"Anyone can have an off-decade."*

...

Daniel Gonzales, knocked out at 2:03 of the first round, on why he didn't know if Sugar Ray Leonard was the best he had ever fought:

> *"I wasn't in there long enough to find out."*

...

Houston Oilers coach Bum Phillips, on the cause of a poor first half:

> *"It was a time mixup. We started playing at 9 o'clock and the kickoff was at 8."*

...

Frank Shorter, on why his winning marathon time of 2:22:44 was a little slower than it could have been:

> *"I would have been 30 seconds faster, but I've been ill and I had to stop to go to the bathroom."*

...

Chuck Cottier, new Seattle Mariners manager, on arriving six days early to spring training:

> *"When you have a one-year contract, you want to stretch that year out as long as possible."*

...

Tennis player John Newcombe, on how he uses tournaments to tell time:

> *"If I'm in the quarterfinals, I know it's Wednesday or Thursday. If I'm in the semifinals, I know it's Saturday. The finals, it's Sunday. But if I get beat in the first round, I go out and get so bloody drunk I don't care what day it is."*

...

Chicago coach Mike Ditka, on the Bears' 10–0 loss to lowly New Orleans just before the start of the 1982 NFL players' strike:

> *"We started the strike yesterday. We're a day ahead of everybody."*

...

Veteran NFL lineman Ron Mix of the Oakland Raiders, explaining where his career was in time:

"You've heard of guys in the twilight of their careers? Well, I'm in the midnight of mine."

...

Catcher Steve Yeager of the Los Angeles Dodgers, who were trailing first-place Cincinnati in the National League (NL) West, explaining time's impact on the pennant race:

"If we don't finish ahead of the Reds, it won't be because we get beat, but just because we run out of time."

...

Former major league player and manager Casey Stengel's philosophy on time:

"There comes a time in every man's life, and I've had plenty of them."

COFFIN CORNER

Who would think that death could serve as an alibi or explanation for the living? It does indeed in this section. As Yogi Berra says, "It's not over 'til it's over." Really over!

... ...

One-time world featherweight champion Willie Pep, on rumors that he had died:

"Naw, I didn't die last night. I wasn't even out of the house."

...

Exercise guru Jack LaLanne, on why he had no plans for dying:

"It would wreck my image. I can't even afford to have a fat dog."

...

Centenary College basketball coach Tommy Canterbury, after a poor defensive effort, on the reason his team's uniforms would include a black patch next season:

"We're going to wear black patches on our jerseys next season because our defense died."

...

New York Times sports columnist Red Smith, on how he had persevered for 50 years in his profession:

"You just don't get dead."

...

Ron Martzoff, WKBW station manager in Buffalo, on why the station elected not to televise games of the dying United States Football League (USFL):

"We don't usually carry funerals."

...

Abe Lemons, University of Texas basketball coach, on the reason he had never caught the jogging bug:

"If I die, I want to be sick."

...

Philadelphia 76ers forward Charles Barkley, on sandbagging on the final lap to fall from third to last place in a two-mile, training-camp run:

"You can't play if you're dead."

...

Eddie "The Eagle" Edwards, British ski jumper and hit of the 1988 Winter Olympics, explaining his goals:

"My goal on every jump is to survive. If I broke a leg, I wouldn't necessarily consider it a bad jump. If I died, that would be bad."

2
Nobody's Perfect

ERRORS OF THEIR PLAY

Okay, so nobody's perfect. But athletes can come up with some real doozies to excuse their mental and official errors. Baseball players seem to be the best at this art, as shown here.

... ...

Eleven-year-old David Frischmann, third baseman for the Dannemora, New York, Red Sox Pee Wees, on the reason a ground ball went through his legs:

"My hands got tongue-tied."

...

New York Mets shortstop Teddy Martinez, on committing five errors in five games:

"I can't play perfect every day."

...

Kansas City shortstop Angel Salazar, on why he let a pop fly drop between him and Royals rookie left-fielder Bo Jackson:

"When I saw Bo, I didn't want to crash into him. If I do that, I'm done playing. My career's over. Hey, my mom still needs me."

...

San Diego Padres outfielder Carmelo Martinez, excusing his defensive play:

"The only problem I really have in the outfield is with fly balls."

RATS, MISSED AGAIN!

Sports would be so boring if athletes made every putt, free throw, field goal, pass reception, and outfield catch. Missing is so much more interesting. There's this burning need to avoid having an albatross with the word "choke" around your neck. So, misses naturally generate some exotic excuses.

... ...

Abe Lemons, Oklahoma City University basketball coach, on the reason his squad goofed up an alley-oop attempt:

"We can alley but we don't have the oop."

...

Centenary College basketball player Barrie Haynie, explaining his shooting woes:

"I sight down my nose to shoot, and now my nose isn't straight since I broke it. That's why my shooting has been off."

...

Chicago White Sox outfielder Ron Kittle, on why he missed a grounder down the left-field line:

"A gopher jumped in front of the ball. It hit him in the head and it went over my glove."

...

JoAnne Carner, on the reason she missed a 6-foot birdie putt while leading the U.S. Women's Open:

"All of a sudden, some streakers went by."

...

Weldon Drew, New Mexico State basketball coach, on why his squad was off to a 1–3 start:

"We have a great bunch of outside shooters. Unfortunately, all our games are played indoors.

...

Seattle SuperSonics guard Bill Hanzlik—knocked silly and fouled on a play—explaining to coach Lenny Wilkens why he missed his two free throws:

"Sorry, but I aimed for the basket in the middle."

...

Kansas Jayhawk basketball player Tony Guy, on his shooting slump:

"I'm trying to do too much and I'm thinking too much, and I'm thinking about trying to do too much."

...

Ted St. Martin, world record holder for consecutive free throws made, on losing to Boston Celtics great and Los Angeles Lakers coach Bill Sharman 90–88 out of 100 free-throw attempts:

"Maybe I was in awe of him."

...

Free-throw shooter extraordinaire Ted St. Martin, on why he had "only" extended his world record to 927 straight free throws:

"I should have had 1,000. I relaxed after 900."

...

National Basketball Association (NBA) Hall of Fame guard Slater Martin, explaining why he opted never to take a chance at perhaps missing a jump shot:

"I couldn't jump."

...

Roger Maltbie, after missing a 2-foot putt at the Greater Hartford Open, on why he blamed a car horn from a nearby street:

"When the horn went off, my hands went off. Once that car horn went 'bingo,' I went with it."

...

New Jersey Net Mike Gminski—an 83 percent career shooter from the charity stripe—offering an analogy for missing three of four free throws in an NBA game:

"Me missing three free throws is like Vanna White turning over the wrong letters."

MAKE NO MISTAKE

Everybody makes mistakes. Athletes are no different, except that their mistakes are much more visible to the world than those of Joe Engineer. Here are some sports figures' reactions and thoughts about blunders, botches, and bungles.

... ...

Auburn running back Bo Jackson, explaining a financial error during a summer stint as a bank teller:

"The first day I was $8,000 short. It was just a rookie mistake."

...

New York catcher Yogi Berra, on the reason the Yankees lost the 1960 World Series to the Pittsburgh Pirates:

"We made too many wrong mistakes."

...

Texas Rangers outfielder Mickey Rivers, explaining his own unique view about mistakes:

"We'll do right if we capitalize on our mistakes."

...

Dallas Cowboys defensive back Charlie Waters, on the potential learning power of his mistakes:

"If I learned by my mistakes, I should be a genius."

...

Bob Goalby, explaining his lack of success on the professional golf tour:

"I don't make mistakes. I make disasters."

...

Georgia Tech football coach Bill Curry, after losing 28–15 to lowly Memphis State:

"There were no coaching mistakes."

CAN'T KICK ABOUT IT

Who is usually the smallest player on a football team? And which player has the most opportunity to be a goat in the last seconds of a tight gridiron clash? Now, if you had to face a whole team of big tough guys after blowing a possible game-winning field goal, what would you do? Right! Make excuses and make them good ones if you want to live.

... ...

Columbia kicker Kurt Dasbach, on blowing a 36-yard field-goal attempt with 19 seconds left that would have snapped the Lions' 39-game losing streak:

"I don't feel like I choked. It was either the wind, or the full moon, or the tides, or gravity, or something."

...

Tampa Bay placekicker Obed Ariri—a Nigerian who went to Clemson—detailing his alibi for failing to explain his missed 42-yard field goal attempt that would have won a game:

"I don't want to talk. I don't speak good English."

...

Ex-NFL kicker and kicking coach Ben Agajanian, relating that some of the best excuses for misses came from the Dallas Cowboys' Rafael Septien:

"He said he missed one kick because the ball was too new. He said he missed another because his helmet was too tight. He missed another because the ball was upside down. We played a game at Canton and he said he missed

because the grass was too high. The next week he missed another field goal. He said, 'Uncle Ben, the grass was too high.' I said, 'Rafael, we're playing on AstroTurf.' "

...

Lou "The Toe" Groza, Hall of Fame placekicker, offering an excuse that all kickers can use:

"Never worry about missing a field goal. Just blame the holder and think about kicking the next one."

THE ANYTHING-GOES DEFENSE

The best defense is a good offense—or was it the best offense is a good defense? No matter. "Winning isn't everything, it's the only thing," as Vince Lombardi once supposedly said. Unless, of course, your team plays lousy defense. Then, it's losing that becomes the only thing. Teams love to play poor defensive teams because almost anything goes . . . for a score, a touchdown, a run, a basket.

... ...

Houston Rockets coach Del Harris, on the difficulty of defending the Denver Nuggets' potent run-and-gun offense:

"Denver doesn't run any plays. That's why they're hard for us to defense."

...

Baltimore Colts coach Frank Kush, explaining why his defense had allowed a long touchdown strike:

"We were in a nickel defense, and it wasn't worth two cents."

San Francisco State basketball coach Lyle Damon, on why the team's opponents had shot only 58 percent from the charity stripe:

"We defend against the free throw very well."

...

Tom Mueller, Texas Christian University (TCU) defensive coordinator, explaining to upset head coach Jim Wacker why no defender was near a receiver who dropped an end-zone pass:

"Coach, if they're not going to catch them, we're not going to cover them."

...

Mark Aguirre, Dallas Mavericks forward, on the reason he had trouble guarding Denver Nuggets forward Kiki Vandeweghe:

"Because he's out of sync. Everything he does seems to be a half-step or half-second different than it should be."

...

Lee Corso, Indiana football coach, gives his alibi for why the low-scoring Hoosiers had given up several long kickoff returns:

"We're not used to kicking off, only returning."

...

Marquette basketball coach Al McGuire, on the reason his teams were involved in so many low-scoring games:

"I couldn't shoot when I played, so I teach defense."

3
Caught in the Act

HELLO, OFFICER

Good afternoon, officer. Nice to see you today. Yeah, right. Quick, think of an excuse! Surprise! Sometimes those officers of the law, who have heard it all before, devise their own excuses for pulling someone over. Here are unique explanations from some officers and from those caught speeding, involved in auto accidents, or who otherwise violated the rules of the road.

... ...

Toni Fritsch, Dallas Cowboys placekicker, on why he picked up a speeding ticket while rushing back to the team's training camp with some food:

"When you eat pizza, it must be warm."

...

Boston Red Sox slugger Dick "Dr. Strangeglove" Stuart, explaining to a police officer—who stopped him on January 2, 1964—why 1963 license plates were still on his car:

"Well, I had such a good year, I didn't want to forget it."

Leon Spinks—after half of his heavyweight boxing title was given to Ken Norton—on why he was arrested for driving without a license and going the wrong way on a one-way street:

"I was celebrating for Norton because he got what he wanted. I got overwhelmed for him."

...

Tommy Lasorda, manager of the Los Angeles Dodgers, on why he was involved in a traffic accident while driving to a press conference to announce his signing for the 1979 season:

"I'm a graduate of the Leon Spinks school of driving."

...

California Highway Patrol officer Phil McHone explaining to Oakland star Reggie Jackson—who had just led the A's to the 1974 World Series title over the Los Angeles Dodgers—why he had been stopped for speeding twice in 20 minutes on I-5 in Southern California's Kern County:

"Reggie, you're in Dodger country."

...

Dennis "Oil Can" Boyd, Boston Red Sox pitcher, after pleading guilty to driving 87 miles per hour in a 55 mile-per-hour zone:

"They [the Red Sox] were complaining about my not getting to the ballpark early, man. All I was trying to do was get to the ballpark early."

...

Lindsey Nelson, New York Mets announcer, on the reason a police officer let him off after stopping him for speeding during the Mets' woeful inaugural season in the majors:

"I said I was a broadcaster for the New York Mets, and he said, 'Buddy, you've got enough troubles.' "

...

Seattle University basketball coach Morris "Bucky" Buckwalter, explaining his auto accident in hoop-ese:

"I set up a moving screen and the other guy ran into it."

...

San Antonio Spur Alfredrick Hughes, on being caught for speeding 128 miles per hour:

"When you're out on the highway, feeling young, strong, and rich, you just can't drive 55."

...

Louisiana State University (LSU) football coach Mike Archer, relating the explanation offered by fullback Victor Jones after being arrested for allegedly driving 123 miles per hour:

"He told me he was just trying to get some bad gas out of his tank."

...

Minnesota Twins manager Billy Gardner, recalling the excuse he used to try to escape a traffic ticket during his playing days with the New York Yankees:

"I was driving to Yankee Stadium and a state trooper stopped me. I told him, 'I'm Billy Gardner, I play for the Yankees, and I'm in a hurry.' The guy said, 'Okay, I'll hurry up and write your ticket.'"

...

An anonymous California Highway patrolman, telling former Boston Celtic Bill Russell why he stopped him for going just over the 55 mile-per-hour speed limit in his Rolls-Royce:

"Well, actually I just wanted to see the inside of your car."

THAT'S AN IMPOSTOR!

Do you ever wish you could impersonate someone for a day? Nobody big, except maybe your boss, the president, Bo Jackson, Joe Montana, or Michael Jordan. Occasionally, the subject of impostors occurs even among athletes. Here are some of the wacky circumstances and the resulting explanations.

... ...

San Diego infielder Kurt Bevacqua—who had previously impersonated Padres manager Dick Williams—on why he could not impersonate then-rotund Los Angeles Dodgers manager Tommy Lasorda:

"Well, I tried to do Tommy Lasorda. But I couldn't find enough pillows to stuff under my shirt."

...

Golfer Johnny Miller, on why he thought changing his swing would snap him out of a slump:

"That hasn't been Johnny Miller out there. That's been somebody else with somebody else's swing."

...

Los Angeles Dodger Mickey Hatcher, on the reason he was wearing ankle weights during spring training:

"I put weights on so when I run sprints I can see what it's like to be [Dodger catcher] Mike Scioscia."

...

Centerfielder Dave Henderson, whose bases-loaded walk gave the Oakland A's a victory, explaining how he once had an even easier RBI:

"The easiest RBI I ever had was when they gave me one of [Seattle Mariner teammate] Steve Henderson's."

CRIME AND PUNISHMENT

A crime against the rules has been committed. Not only that, but the perpetrator has been caught. Here are excuses designed in an attempt to escape punishment from the authorities.

... ...

Minnesota Twins manager Gene Mauch, after being ejected for arguing and then tossing bats onto the field, on the excuse he would use to ward off a possible fine by the commissioner:

"I'll just say I was taking the bats home and they slipped out of my hands."

Oakland Raiders defensive tackle John Matuszak, fined
$1,000 for a team curfew violation, on why he was out
at a nightclub at 3:00 A.M.:

*"I am the enforcer. That's why I was out on the
streets—to make sure no one else was."*

...

Green Bay defensive back Erza Johnson, who was fined $1,000 for eating a hot dog on the sidelines during a 38–0 exhibition-game loss, on his rationale:

"It would have been different if I had eaten that thing because we were losing, or because of disrespect. I ate it because I was hungry."

RULES ARE MADE
TO BE BROKEN

Rules, rules, rules. Can't live without 'em, can't live with 'em! For example, it is prudent for society to set speed-limit rules, but who hasn't broken these rules at some time despite this understanding! For athletes, it is most prudent to know and follow the rules. Pity the poor coaches who must set the rules that will most likely be broken by some player. Following the rules may actually be easier than establishing them—at least most of the time.

... ...

Steve Wilson, Dallas Cowboys punt returner, on his failure to down the ball instead of running a muffed punt out of the end zone and getting tackled at the 4-yard line:

"I didn't know the rule and I didn't have time to look it up."

...

Abe Lemons, Oklahoma City University basketball coach, on why he wasn't crazy about having team rules:

"If I make a set of rules, then a guy goes out and

steals an airplane. He comes back and says, 'It wasn't on the list of rules.' "

...

Frank McGuire, South Carolina basketball coach, asked to elaborate on his training rules:

"My training rule is 'don't get caught.' "

...

Arnold Palmer, on whether he ever walked out on a golf tournament without a good excuse:

"Not since it has been against the rules."

...

An anonymous Soviet spokesman, on the reason rule enforcement was sometimes lax at the 1986 Goodwill Games in Moscow compared to other international competitions:

"In an atmosphere of goodwill and cooperation, we decided to violate some of the rules."

PLAYING THEM FOR PATSIES

Coaches want to keep their jobs. The best way to accomplish job security is to win. Of course, it never hurts to stack the deck in your favor! And college coaches do. Play a patsy, pick up an easy "W." Everyone goes home happy. Unfortunately, sometimes the tables are turned as your team winds up as the patsy of a powerhouse school. Look, coach, at least your school is guaranteed a fat payday for taking your licks!

... ...

Iowa basketball coach George Raveling, on why accusations that he scheduled too many weak opponents didn't concern him:

"I know a lot of coaches who loaded up with powerhouses who are now working at K mart."

...

Tay Baker, Xavier of Ohio hoop coach, on charges his team has a patsy schedule:

"It's a lot easier to justify a schedule than to justify a loss."

...

Frank Broyles, Arkansas football coach, justifying soft schedules:

"A team that is overscheduled begins to lose. Then it loses its fans, its players—and then its coach."

...

Georgia Tech football coach Pepper Rodgers, tells his alibi for being routed 31–7 by Notre Dame:

"I didn't schedule them."

...

Stan Morrison, University of Southern California (USC) basketball coach, on why he didn't put Pepperdine on the Trojans' schedule:

"We don't want to lose to them."

...

Indiana football coach Lee Corso, on the reason he added the USC Trojans to the Hoosiers' schedule:

"When I took this job I promised our fans I'd show them a Rose Bowl team."

...

Peter Gavett, Maine basketball coach, explaining a season-opening 115–57 loss to Virginia and 7'4" center Ralph Sampson:

"I think this whole game hinged on one call— the one I made last April scheduling the game."

4
Well, You See, It's Like This ...

IN-DEPTH ANALYSIS

To explain success or failure sometimes calls for a closer, analytical examination of the specific situation. That's no problem for some. But for others, watch out! The floodgates open and the river of analysis flows. Making *sense* out of that analysis, however, is a totally different thing.

... ...

Baltimore Oriole outfielder John Lowenstein, and his analysis of winning streaks:

> *"The secret to keeping winning streaks going is to maximize the victories while, at the same time, minimizing the defeats."*

...

Minnesota manager Tom Kelly, after Twins starting pitcher Les Straker was strafed for four runs in one-third of an inning:

> *"He just didn't seem like he was into the game. Maybe his biorhythms were off."*

32

Mike Hargrove of the Cleveland Indians, explaining the magic .300 mark:

"Everybody likes to be known as a .300 hitter. If you hit .299, nobody remembers you as a .300 hitter."

...

Cleveland Browns coach Sam Rutigliano, over-explaining a defeat:

"If you can't make the putts and can't get the man in from second in the bottom of the ninth, you're not going to win enough football games in this league and that's the problem we had today."

...

Kansas City Royals pitcher Rich Gale, analyzing his early knockout by the Seattle Mariners:

"I was super in the first inning. In the second inning, I eroded in parts, and in the third inning I completely disappeared."

...

San Diego pitcher Eric Show, on pitching and results:

"You can pitch a gem and lose, but you can't lose when you win . . . wait, don't quote me on that. I sound like Yogi Berra."

...

New Jersey guard Otis Birdsong, on why the Nets had lost an NBA contest:

"I think we played hard, but it was a lackadaisical hard."

...

Lee Trevino, on his 78 during the third round of the
PGA Championship tournament:

*"I cut enough hay out there to feed all the cows
in Texas."*

...

Oakland manager Tony La Russa, explaining the A's slow start during the 1987 season:

"When you're not winning, it's tough to win a game."

...

Deion Sanders became the first player ever to hit a home run in the major leagues and return a punt for a touchdown in an NFL game in the same week. Several months before accomplishing this feat, Sanders explained the reason he would rather return a punt for a touchdown than hit a home run:

"That counts six points. The homer only counts for one."

...

When Utah coach Frank Layden asked Jazz forward Jeff Wilkens whether his poor performance in a game was due to ignorance or apathy, Layden said he received this explanation:

"Coach, I don't know and I don't care."

BECAUSE, BECAUSE

Have you ever met a little kid who likes to ask a lot of questions? In a row. For hours. *Why do I have to go to bed now?* Because you have to. *Because why?* Because I say so. *Because why?* And on and on. You know the kid. It's funny how many adults utilize the way of their childhood to make excuses.

... ...

Ohio State secondary coach Lou Holtz, asked by head
coach Woody Hayes why O. J. Simpson had gone 80
yards for a touchdown in the 1969 Rose Bowl:

"Because that's all he needed, coach."

...

NL president A. Bartlett Giamatti, on why so many
balks were being called during the 1987 season:

*"I asked Ed Vargo of our umpiring staff and he
said it was because pitchers were committing
more balks this season."*

...

Galveston, Texas, police officer Paul Millo, on the
reason officers had to pull guns on shot-putter Brian
Oldfield during a nightclub incident:

"Because nightsticks didn't affect him."

...

Seattle Mariners manager Dick Williams, on not going
"by the book":

*"I don't manage by the book because I've never
met the guy who wrote it."*

...

Relief pitcher Al Hrabosky, after inking a $5.9 million
pact with the Atlanta Braves, explaining why he was
worth that much money:

"Because they're paying it to me."

...

Detroit coach Monte Clark, with his alibi after his lowly Lions blew a 14–0 first quarter lead and lost to Buffalo, 20–17:

"We don't know how to protect a lead, because we haven't had one very often."

...

Betty Cook, U.S. offshore-boat-racing champion, on the reason her sport lacks prize money:

"Because there aren't bleachers between here [Los Angeles] and Catalina [Island]."

...

Dave Garcia, interim Cleveland Indians manager, explaining why the team won its first seven games under him:

"The only reason we're 7–0 is because we've won all seven of our games."

...

Owner Ted Turner, suspended for managing an Atlanta Braves game during a 14-game losing streak, asked by Commissioner Bowie Kuhn why he couldn't be like other owners:

"Because I'm in last place."

IF . . .

If this had happened and that hadn't happened, then our team would have won! Yeah, sure. If you believe that, there's some choice swampland in Florida I want to sell you. It turns out that the word *if* is actually a popular excuse for just about anything.

... ...

Golfer Mike Reid, on why he hit his ball into the lake on the 18th hole at the U.S. Open:

"If I had known it was going in the water, I wouldn't have hit it there."

...

Yogi Berra, explaining to Los Angeles Dodger executive Al Campanis why his team's loss in a minor-league playoff series to an opposing team that included Campanis wasn't really a loss:

"You wouldn't have won it if we had beaten you."

...

George Bamberger, Milwaukee Brewers manager, after a tough loss by one of his pitchers:

"He's pitched three or four games where, if we'd scored more runs for him, he would have won."

...

New York Mets pitcher Ron Darling, after watching new teammate Don Schulze walk on four pitches, recalled that he once gave Schulze an intentional pass:

"Now, I know he can't hit. If I'd known that then, I wouldn't have walked him."

...

Bart Starr, Green Bay Packers head coach, explaining a loss:

"Except for three big plays, we played well enough to win, if we had been able to do anything on offense."

...

St. Louis manager Whitey Herzog, who guided his team over San Francisco in the NL playoffs, explaining why the Cardinals lost in seven games to Minnesota in the 1987 World Series:

> *"To beat the Giants without Jack Clark and take the Minnesota Twins to the seventh game without Terry Pendleton and Jack Clark—if we'd played four games in St. Louis instead of four games in Minnesota, we'd have kicked their tails."*

...

H. K. "Cootie" Reeves, Hokes Bluff (Alabama) High School football coach, after his team received a 53–0 lashing from Hazlewood in the state Double A title game:

> *"If we hadn't given them those first four touchdowns, it might have been different."*

STAND UP, SIT DOWN

To sit or not to sit, that is the question! At high school football games, energetic cheerleaders enthusiastically exhort their student bodies to "stand up, sit down, fight, fight, fight!" thus covering both sides of the question. Here are some explanations involving the art of sitting down or standing up.

... ...

Clemson athletic director Frank Howard, on the reason he nixed a request that the university field a crew team:

> *"We ain't gonna have no sport where you sit down and go backwards."*

...

Hubert Green, 1976 PGA money-leader, explaining why he had yet to win a major tournament:

"Every time it's come to stand up and be counted, I've sat down."

...

Former Green Bay Packers receiver Max McGee, explaining how tough coach Vince Lombardi was:

"When he said 'sit down,' I didn't even bother to look for a chair."

...

Gary Williams, American University basketball coach, on why the playground is the best place to learn hoops:

"Because if you lose, you sit down."

5
The Wacky
And Offbeat

COLORFUL ANALOGIES

The art of making excuses can really flourish when the old imagination kicks into high gear. Offering alibis by way of analogy takes brains and knowledge of a world outside sports. Here are some choice analogies that may provide inspiration during those rare occasions of temporary setbacks at work, home, or on the athletic field.

... ...

Dennis Harrison, 6'8", 275-pound Philadelphia Eagles rookie defensive end, on why he thought he was passed over until the fourth round in the NFL draft:

> *"The scouts said I looked like Tarzan and played like Jane."*

...

Fred Taylor, Ohio State basketball coach, explaining the Buckeyes' 80–66 loss to North Carolina in the

National Collegiate Athletic Association (NCAA) tournament semifinals:

> *"They called us the Cinderella team and we played like we were going to turn into a pumpkin."*

...

Wake Forest football coach Chuck Mills, on why his team had only gradually improved its record from 1–9–1 to 5–6 over four seasons:

> *"We're a glacier, not an avalanche."*

...

Pro golfer Chi Chi Rodriguez, analyzing an up-and-down round:

> *"I played like Doug Sanders and putted like Colonel Sanders."*

...

Florida assistant football coach Doug Knotts, after the Gators' upset loss to North Carolina:

> *"We have snap and crackle linebackers. What we need is pop."*

...

New York Knicks guard Walt Frazier, on why Jerry Sloan of the Chicago Bulls is such a tough defensive guard:

> *"When you're playing him it's like going through the tunnel of love. All you feel is hands, knees, and elbows all over you."*

...

Oakland A's relief pitcher Bill Caudill, reflecting on an off-day on the mound:

"Even Betty Crocker burns a cake now and then."

...

Ohio State running back Archie Griffin, on how he won two Heisman Trophies despite his 5'9", 182-pound frame:

"It's not the size of the dog in the fight, but the size of the fight in the dog."

...

Jim Dent, the PGA Tour's longest hitter, on why his drives were sometimes lacking in accuracy:

"I can airmail the golf ball, but sometimes I don't put the right address on it."

...

Chicago Cubs right fielder Bobby Murcer, on his excuse for struggling against Atlanta Braves knuckleballer Phil Niekro:

"Trying to hit him is like trying to eat Jell-O with chopsticks."

...

University of Kansas football coach Don Fambrough, explaining spring practice:

"You never know if it's good or bad. It's like having a daughter coming in at four in the morning carrying a Gideon Bible."

...

Kermit Davis, Mississippi State basketball coach, on his squad's midseason turnover-itis:

"I know we're making some mistakes because we're young. But every once in a while, we play as wild as dirt-road lizards."

...

Notre Dame football coach Lou Holtz, on why he prefers competence to experience:

"I don't want the kamikaze pilot who flew 54 different missions. I want somebody who can get it right the first time."

...

Oakland owner Charlie Finley, on how he operates the A's:

"We run our club like a pawnshop—we buy, we trade, we sell."

...

Mychal Thompson, Los Angeles Laker backup center, on the reason he didn't respond in kind after being nailed by Kareem Abdul-Jabbar's elbow during practice:

"You don't elbow the King. If you elbow the King, they throw you in the dungeon."

...

Chi Chi Rodriguez, explaining how he felt after shooting a round of 76 to drop six strokes off the lead in the PGA Seniors Championship:

"Yesterday, I felt like I was the best player in the world. Today, I felt like Tiny Tim."

...

Chuck Mills, Wake Forest football coach, after his perennial cellar-dweller team trounced Virginia, 66–21:

"Oh, we've always seen the light at the end of the tunnel. We just weren't sure whether it was a light or our house burning down."

The Charlotte Hornets' Robert Reid, explaining his thoughts at first seeing teammate Kurt Rambis attired in the team's designer uniform:

"It was like a construction worker putting on a tuxedo to go watch Pavarotti."

...

Seattle Seahawks linebacker Brian Bosworth, on his slow recovery from a shoulder injury:

"It's like shopping with your grandmother. You hurry up and wait."

...

Ben Jobe, Southern University basketball coach, after being scalped 126–81 by the St. John's Redmen:

"We tried to play a fast-paced game, but you can't control the Redmen. Custer found that out."

...

San Diego Padres pitcher Bruce Hurst—who came to the National League after spending his entire career in the American League with its designated-hitter rule—explaining how he managed to get his first major league hit:

"Even a blind dog finds a bone every once in a while."

...

Pete Gillen, Xavier basketball coach, explaining his role in society:

"I'm just a caraway seed in the bakery of life."

IT'S OFF-THE-WALL

Part of the fun of sports is its characters. The sports world's penchant for wacky behavior and remarks offers the fan a distinct contrast from the sometimes staid stuffiness of the typical workplace where conformity is the rule. Here are some offbeat excuses, alibis, and explanations from that more interesting world of off-the-wall characters.

... ...

Rocky Bridges, manager in the Carolina League, on his runner-up finish in a milking contest:

"I didn't try too hard. I was afraid I'd get emotionally involved with the cow."

...

Muffin Spencer-Devlin, professional golfer and believer in reincarnation, explaining why she occasionally walks backward:

"It's to strengthen my quadriceps. In my next life I'm going to be a downhill racer."

...

Darryl Dawkins of the Philadelphia 76ers, offering his explanation after shattering the backboard glass during an NBA game:

"It was the power, the chocolate thunder. I could feel it surging through my body, fighting to get out. I had no control over it."

...

San Francisco manager Charlie Fox, on the reason he salaamed to Giants pitcher Ron Bryant, who had just blanked the Chicago Cubs:

"He complained that I didn't shake his hand after he won a game, so I told him if it would help, I'd get down on my knees and bow three times."

...

African witch doctor John Agunga, on why his spells failed to provide the Baltimore Orioles with the American League East Division title:

"Publicity. They lost because they turned coming to me into a publicity gimmick. Witchcraft works only by stealth."

...

San Jose Bees catcher Darryl Cias, on his motivation for painting Charles Manson's picture on the team's locker-room door:

"I thought it might brighten up the place."

...

Basketball coach Nob Scott, watching his Cal State–Los Angeles squad en route to a ninth consecutive loss, explaining why he joined Cal Poly–Pomona coach Don Hogan on the opposition bench:

"I just wanted to see what it feels like to be on the winning side. I'd forgotten."

...

Rice basketball coach Don Knodel, with his Owls trailing Arkansas by 20 points late in the game, on why he decided to go sit on the Razorbacks' bench:

"I wanted to be on the winning bench."

Tanzanian Filbert Bayi, 1,500-meter world-record-holder, on how he managed to win his first 5,000-meter race against major competition:

> *"I'm building my own house in Tanzania, but thieves have been carrying away the lumber all the time. So I've been running longer to hunt the thieves."*

...

Promoter Dick Meek, on the reason given by boxer Zip Castillo for canceling a scheduled welterweight fight against Pat Hallacy:

> *"He said he dreamed he'd been knocked out in the fight and didn't wake up. He thought it was a bad omen and didn't want to fight."*

...

World-class sprinter Charlie Greene of the University of Nebraska, on why he wore sunglasses even at night track meets:

> *"Man, they're not shades. They're my re-entry shields."*

...

Richie Hebner, Philadelphia Phillies first baseman, explaining why he enjoys his off-season job as a gravedigger:

> *"You can't beat the peace and quiet around a cemetery."*

...

Boxer Joe Frazier, on the reason he hadn't been his usual bubbly, enthusiastic self:

"I had the slouchies and when you're feeling slouchy, there's no sense trying to fight your way out of them. Just let things go."

...

Michigan's Garde Thompson, after erupting for a career-high 33 points against Navy in the NCAA basketball tournament, on his difficulty in supplying a urine sample for an NCAA postgame drug test:

"I couldn't go. It was the only thing I couldn't fill up all night."

...

Boston Red Sox outfielder Jim Rice, on the reason he didn't want to serve as the team's captain:

"Captains go down with the ship."

...

Darryl Dawkins, explaining why he wore number 53 with both the Philadelphia 76ers and New Jersey Nets:

"It's my birthday. I was born on the 53rd of November."

...

Minnesota Twins manager Billy Gardner, on a good excuse a minor-league player once offered for being unable to depart for two days after being sent down:

"He told me he had a second-floor apartment and a waterbed that would take two days to drain. I went over there that night, and sure enough, there was a hose coming from his bedroom window and water spilling all over the place."

...

North Carolina Wesleyan basketball guard Jeff Hood, telling coach John McCarthy why he slept through the morning instead of studying:

"Coach, my books are asleep, too."

6
Double-Play Gripes: Losing and the Officials

LOSING IT

Individuals deal with losing in slightly different ways. Some deny it. Some downplay it. Some dispute it. Some explain it. Some excuse it. Yes, for every winner there is a loser. But which of those two sides has the more creative and interesting postcompetition comments? Here are some of the losers' excuses and alibis.

... ...

An optimistic Gilbert Alvarez, North Dallas, Texas, High School girls' basketball coach, explaining a 136–7 loss to South Oak Cliffs:

"We just need to work on some fundamentals."

...

Houston coach Bum Phillips, on why the Oilers were trounced 34–5 by the Pittsburgh Steelers:

"The harder we played, the behinder we got."

Tennis pro Bob Lutz, excusing himself for falling to Guillermo Vilas in a World Championship Tennis match:

"I got tired, my ears started popping, the rubber came off my tennis shoes, I got a cramp, and I lost one of my contact lenses. Other than that, I was in great shape."

...

Ken Hayes, basketball coach at Oral Roberts University, on the reason his team lost to Oklahoma State by just two points after trailing by 13 points at halftime:

"We just dug ourselves a 10-foot hole, then dug out 9 feet, 11 inches."

...

Joaquim Cruz, 1984 Olympic 800-meter champion from Brazil, explaining why he didn't really lose to American miler Steve Scott in a U.S. distance race decided by a photo finish:

"If that race was in Brazil, I win."

...

Joe Jacobs, manager of heavyweight champion Max Schmeling, after Jack Sharkey won a controversial 15-round decision to take the title:

"We wuz robbed."

...

Cleveland guard World B. Free, after officials didn't call an apparent charge against Boston's Larry Bird late in the game, on why the Cavaliers lost to the Celtics:

"We were cheated."

...

Wimbledon champion Margaret Court, after losing to 55-year-old Bobby Riggs in a "Battle of the Sexes" tennis match:

"He messed me around and upset my normal style of play . . . It was all a bit sneaky."

...

Denver center Danny Schayes, on why the Nuggets fell to the Golden State Warriors:

"They got a lot of long rebounds. Well, actually, they got every rebound."

...

San Diego Clippers forward Terry Cummings, explaining a 17-point loss to the Dallas Mavericks:

"We were a little sluggish—no, we were a lot sluggish."

...

Rice football coach Jess Neely, on his team's 24–0 loss to Georgia Tech:

"I think we oversold the boys on their steady play the week before against Louisiana Tech; against Tech they were about stationary."

...

Boston Celtics coach Bill Fitch, explaining a seventh game loss to the Philadelphia 76ers in an NBA playoff series:

"There were enough bad passes and missed free throws to knock out any theories about coaching being responsible."

...

Oklahoma football coach Barry Switzer, after losing to Miami for the national title, on why the Sooners had a three-game losing streak against the Hurricanes:

"It's not that they've got better players. It's the system. Their offensive line isn't better than ours. They've got a quarterback and wide receivers. That's what beat us."

C. M. Newton, longtime Vanderbilt basketball coach, explaining a loss to Auburn:

"A lot of bad things happened to us. First, Auburn played well."

...

Bill Mallory, Northern Illinois football coach, on the reasons for a nauseating 31–6 loss to Northwestern that shattered the Wildcats' 34-game losing streak:

"Our kicking game stunk. Our offense stunk. Our defense stunk. We stunk."

...

Jim Valvano, on why his North Carolina State squad was ousted from the Atlantic Coast Conference postseason tournament by rival North Carolina:

"In this league, everybody gets ready for the league games and the tournament. We peaked for the Polish National team in November."

...

Houston Rockets guard Mike Newlin, explaining a loss to the New York Nets:

"We were the quintessence of atrocity."

...

TCU basketball coach Buster Brannon—whose Horned Frogs had bad records after moving into a new pavilion—explaining to another coach why he shouldn't be in a hurry to build a new gym:

"That way you lose your alibi."

...

Sam Wyche, Cincinnati Bengals coach, on the reason girls, beaches, and sun were the causes behind the Bengals' 21–13 exhibition loss at Tampa Bay:

"You get down there, you see all the girls out on the beach in the nice, warm weather, and it's just not a football atmosphere."

...

Jack Hartman, Kansas State basketball coach, on how the Wildcats melted away a 14-point lead and lost to Iowa State:

"Our wings began to ice."

...

Larry Jones, fired as Florida State football coach after an 0–11 season, on the reason for all that losing:

"That opening loss to Wake Forest hurt our confidence."

...

Bob Weltlich, Texas basketball coach, on his alibi for an 84–67 defeat against Arkansas:

"They dribble faster than we run without the ball."

...

Iowa football coach Hayden Fry, on why Big Ten Conference teams, which mostly play on artificial turf, had so much trouble winning the Rose Bowl against Pacific-10 Conference teams, which mostly play on grass:

"Every time we go out to play on the West Coast, we look like we're running in mud and it looks like they're on skateboards."

Milwaukee manager Harvey Kuehn, on why the Cardinals' artificial surface was the reason his Brewers lost to St. Louis in the seventh game of the 1982 World Series:

"Had we played Game 7 in Milwaukee, it would have been a different story. The first three hits St. Louis got off us that last game would have been easy groundballs on any grass surface. The experts told me that seven of the base hits St. Louis got in that game were AstroTurf hits. We got one."

...

Texas basketball coach Abe Lemons, on the reason his squad fell to Arkansas 72–61 in a rough Southwest Conference game:

"They had more first downs than we did."

...

Edwin Moses, on why his last loss before the start of his 10-year, 107-race winning streak in the 400-meter hurdles came in a European race against West German Harald Schmid:

"I'd run three races in five days, stayed up late, and I was staying with this guy who had a big mansion, Rolls-Royce service to the track, swimming pool in the basement. I was out there eating cookies and tea on the porch when I should have been going to the track. I just got caught off guard."

...

California football coach Joe Kapp, explaining a 24–17 loss to Oregon:

> *"We relaxed and I don't coach that. You're supposed to relax after the game, and I coach that real good."*

IT'S ALL THE REF'S FAULT!

"Now this late report from the stadium. The argument between the two baseball teams continued into its third hour as neither side budged over the disputed close play at the plate." Without officials, sports contests might become like United Nations debates that go on and on. With the authority bestowed upon them by their league offices, officials have the authority and power to make the calls, continue the game, and avoid anarchy. In return, officials are the most convenient target for blame when their decisions don't go the way the losing team's players, coaches, and fans would have liked. Here are some excuses and explanations involving the officials.

... ...

Tommy Canterbury, Centenary College basketball coach, explaining his thoughts about the officiating, after a loss:

> *"The trouble with the officials is, they just don't care who wins."*

...

Jim Finks, general manager of the New Orleans Saints, on why he couldn't talk about controversial calls:

> *"We're not allowed to comment on lousy officiating."*

...

Pro tennis player Pam Teeguarden, after losing a match, on why she felt the linespeople had been against her:

"I have to be honest. I think I lost because I wasn't wearing a bra."

...

Ohio State basketball coach Fred Taylor, on why he could stand for one minute at midcourt and not receive a technical foul while Indiana coach Bobby Knight got nailed for two technicals just for sighing:

"Bobby sighs a little more profanely than I do."

...

Cincinnati Stingers coach Terry Slater, reasoning why a touring squad from the Soviet Union beat his World Hockey Association team, 7–5:

"If the officiating had been honest, we would have won."

...

NBA referee Earl Strom, during a time-out at an Indiana Pacers game, asked by an elderly woman why he was watching a "disgusting" display on the court by four topless women publicizing a local nightclub:

"Madame, I am trying to determine exactly how disgusting it is."

...

Tampa Bay assistant coach Dennis Fryzel, trying to make an excuse to an official after the Buccaneers were penalized for 12 men on the field:

"Okay, which one was it?"

...

Florida State basketball coach Hugh Durham, after a loss to New Mexico, explaining how he would overcome the poor officiating next time:

> *"They let people jump over the backs of players to rebound. I'm sure if we took trampoline lessons for a couple of weeks we could adjust to the officiating."*

...

NL umpire Stan Landes, on why he ejected Los Angeles Dodger shortstop Maury Wills for arguing that San Francisco Giant Bobby Bonds had interfered with first baseman Wes Parker:

> *"He didn't have a good view of the game, so I gave him a chance to watch the end of it on television."*

...

Iowa State basketball coach Johnny Orr, explaining why he was going to keep quiet following a 73–70 loss to Missouri that saw the Tigers shoot 35 free throws to his Cyclones' nine attempts:

> *"I'm not going to say anything about the officiating, because it might take two days."*

...

Buffalo coach Chuck Knox, on why he thought the Bills racked up 134 yards in penalties while losing to Detroit, 28–20:

> *"Maybe the officials wanted to get some practice throwing flags."*

...

Kareem Abdul-Jabbar, Los Angeles Lakers center, after establishing an NBA career record of 4,194 fouls:

"Half of them were bad calls."

...

Houston Astros pitcher Nolan Ryan, explaining how he managed to establish the major-league career record for allowing the most walks:

"I never would have been able to do it without the umpires."

...

Indiana coach Bobby Knight, on the reason he was banished from a game in the Collegiate Commissioners Association basketball tournament, a consolation event to the NCAA championships in the 1970s:

"I wasn't trying to arouse anybody, but we had here a consolation tournament so we got stuck with consolation officials."

...

Tennessee Tech football coach Don Wade, who claimed he hadn't criticized officials in 30 years, on the quality of officiating in his team's 21–0 road loss to Cameron (Oklahoma):

"I suspect they got some of them officials in the downtown pool hall. They were a bunch of damned crooks."

...

Philadelphia 76ers center Moses Malone, recalling the reason for the last time he fouled out:

"Cheap call."

...

Butch Beard, New York Knicks assistant coach, on the local cause of the team's struggling season:

> *"Night in and night out we have to score 10 field goals more just to make it close. I blame the press. If we don't get any respect here, why should we get it from the officials?"*

...

Kansas coach Larry Brown, explaining why official Jim Bain tagged him with a technical foul during the Big Eight basketball tournament:

> *"It goes back to when I was at UCLA and we had him against Notre Dame. He was looking to put a technical on me all day."*

...

Baltimore Orioles manager Earl Weaver, on the reason he had so many arguments with umpires:

> *"If you do the screaming, the players won't. If you get thrown out, they won't. You've got to keep ballplayers in the lineup."*

7
Social Disgraces

LEWD, CRUDE, AND RUDE

Occasionally the colorful world of sports competition may become off-color. This most often results in disgraceful exhibitions toward the officials or the fans. Despite their obvious guilt for rude conduct, the ill-mannered louts will make up some feeble excuse to justify their behavior.

... ...

Philadelphia 76er Darryl Dawkins, after his ejection from a game against the Houston Rockets for allegedly making an obscene gesture at official Darell Garretson:

"I was just adjusting my athletic supporter."

...

Chub Feeney, who resigned as general manager of the San Diego Padres after an incident with fans at Jack Murphy Stadium, explaining his version:

"I deny giving an obscene gesture. I was just waving."

...

Soccer referee Jorge Regueira, after his arrest in Montevideo, Uruguay, for making obscene gestures to the crowd during a game:

"I was only fixing the zipper on my pants."

...

Paul Cannell, forward for the Washington Diplomats of the North American Soccer League, on why he protested an official's call by dropping his shorts:

"I was just trying to give the league a little exposure."

BETTER LATE THAN NEVER

The world likes to run on time. But who hasn't been late at one time or another? To soothe the waiting party requires the invention of a somewhat plausible, but mostly lame, excuse. That opportunity to express such originality is part of the fun of being late! Here are some lame excuses concocted by sports figures to explain their tardiness.

... ...

Brook Steppe of the Indiana Pacers, on why he missed a team flight that required his awakening by 7:30 A.M.:

"Sometime during the night, I accidentally hit my alarm clock and knocked it upside down. So, when it went off, I thought it was only 10 after two."

...

Outfielder Claudell Washington had a brief explanation for taking four days to report to the Chicago White Sox after being traded by the Texas Rangers:

"I overslept."

...

Tennis pro Arthur Ashe, on his late arrival at the lavish estate of millionaire Lamar Hunt:

"I couldn't find Lamar's home even after I got inside the gate."

...

Cotton Fitzsimmons, just after he was fired as coach of the Atlanta Hawks, on the reason for his late arrival at a post-firing press conference:

"I didn't realize how many people there were in the unemployment lines."

...

George Foster, New York Mets outfielder, with his unusual alibi for being late to spring training in Florida:

"It was cold in Connecticut and raining on Maui."

...

Former Philadelphia slugger Dick Allen, on why he declined the Phillies' invitation to play in an Old-Timers Game:

"I'd probably be late for it and get fined again."

...

Stan Greeson, Harlem Globetrotters president, on the reason he failed to make a luncheon appointment:

"My social schedule was being handled by Duane Thomas."

...

Heisman Trophy winner Johnny Rodgers, on why he was late for a San Diego Chargers practice:

"A man in my position can't help but be tardy sometimes."

...

New York Yankee outfielder Mickey Rivers—after reaching agreement a day earlier on a million-dollar, three-year contract extension—on why he was late for a spring training session:

"Tax problems."

...

Ohio State coach Woody Hayes, on why he made reporters wait for one hour before letting them enter the locker room after a game against Minnesota:

"I had a whole room full of recruits and when you have to choose between a room full of recruits and a room full of writers, you talk to the recruits."

...

Umpire Augie Donatelli, explaining to New York Mets manager Yogi Berra why it took him so long to call a foul tip:

"I was waiting to hear it."

DIRTY PLAY

Some players are so clean you could eat off their uniforms. Then there are others—such as Ty Cobb and Dick Butkus—who gained somewhat rotten reputations on the field. Here are some excuses from the mean and dirty side of sports.

... ...

Chicago Bears lineman William "The Refrigerator" Perry, on why he threw St. Louis Cardinals quarterback Neil Lomax to the ground after lifting him shoulder-high into the air:

"If I let him go, he could have thrown a touchdown pass."

...

George Steinbrenner, on the reason his horse—a 29–1 longshot named Steve's Friend—lost the 1977 Kentucky Derby to Seattle Slew:

"My horse was running well, but at one point on the track they used some darker dirt to cover a wet spot or something. When my horse and another horse got there, they jumped the darker dirt and lost stride."

...

Chicago Bears linebacker Dick Butkus, explaining that he wasn't a dirty player:

"I never set out to hurt anybody deliberately unless it was, you know, important—like a league game or something."

...

Joseph Csonka, father of tough Miami Dolphins fullback Larry Csonka, explaining his son's meanness:

"I can remember hearing our dog bark, going outside and seeing three-year-old Larry with one of the dog's legs in his mouth. I'd ask him what he was doing and he'd say, 'Well, he bit me first.'"

...

New York Giants tackle Charlie Harper, on how to stop the ferocious pass rush of All-Pro defensive end Bubba Smith of the Baltimore Colts:

"Get down low and tie his shoelaces together."

...

Mike Ditka, when he was a Dallas Cowboys tight end, on his mean reputation:

"I'm not mean at all. I just try to protect myself, and you'll notice I don't ever pick on anybody who has a number above 30."

RIP CITY

Okay, okay, so some cities have their faults. Doesn't every city? You don't have to be so critical, you creep! Why don't you get out of town while the getting out is good? And, by the way, don't ever come back! If, by some chance, you do come back, we'll be waiting for you, won't we, boys?

... ...

After being traded from the Cleveland Indians to the Cincinnati Reds to replace Pete Rose at third base, Buddy Bell explained why he could bear the pressure:

"Nobody knows pressure until they've played in Cleveland for seven years."

...

LaVell Edwards, Brigham Young University football coach, on his team's 33–20 loss to Wyoming during a snowstorm at the Cowboys' War Memorial Stadium in Laramie:

"I'd rather lose and live in Provo than win and live in Laramie."

Martina Navratilova, on why she was happy to be with the Boston Lobsters of World Team Tennis after playing for the Cleveland Nets:

"There's too much pollution in Cleveland."

...

Offensive lineman Tony Mandarich, Green Bay Packer first-round draft pick, excusing himself for making some derogatory comments about Green Bay during his contract holdout:

"I did call Green Bay a village, in Playboy, *but every village needs a village idiot."*

...

Dallas Mavericks coach Dick Motta, explaining exactly how small his hometown of Union, Utah, was:

"It was so small we didn't have a village idiot. My brother and I had to take turns."

MODESTY, ANYONE?

When's the last time you heard about a modest athlete? Sure, athletes need to be confident, and maybe a little bit of cockiness doesn't hurt. If you have the credentials to back up the reason for your cockiness, then it can be a case of "No brag, just fact." Here are some "modest" quotes from the world of sports.

... ...

Muhammad Ali, on whether he ever experienced a modest moment:

"When you're so good, it's hard to be humble."

...

71

USC football coach John McKay, on the reason his vote for No. 1 went to Alabama instead of to his Trojans:

"I'm so damn modest."

...

Chicago Cubs pitcher Dennis Lamp, on why a pendant he wore was engraved with the number 15:

"Because on a scale of one to 10, I'm a 15."

...

Andy Van Slyke, Pittsburgh Pirates outfielder, explaining who he would choose to change places with out of anyone in the world:

"My wife, so I could see how wonderful it is to live with me."

...

Pittsburgh Pirates slugger Dave Parker, on why he wore the Star of David on one of his necklaces:

"I'm David and I'm a star."

8
Playing with Emotion

NERVOUS NELLIES

Every athlete has felt the old butterflies before the start of competition. But other things besides competition can make some athletes high-strung. Here are several excuses for such behavior.

... ...

Eddie Dibbs, on why he was so nervous in the first set of his 4–6, 6–0, 6–1 victory over Rod Laver:

"I used to be a ballboy for him."

...

North Carolina State center Chuck Nevitt, explaining to coach Jim Valvano why he looked nervous during a practice session:

"My sister's expecting a baby and I don't know if I'm going to be an uncle or an aunt."

...

73

A very nervous San Francisco pitcher Mike LaCoss, during a Los Angeles earthquake, explaining to Giants travel director Dirk Smith why his hotel accommodations were unsatisfactory:

"You've got to get me a new room. This one's shaking."

THE FEAR FACTOR

As spectators, it is often easy to forget that sport can sometimes be dangerous. A blowout at high speed during a stock car race, a 100 mile-per-hour fastball zeroing in on one's head, a near-fall during a downhill ski race at 80 miles per hour, or a blind-side sack of the quarterback by a 300-pound defensive lineman can all get the heart pounding and the adrenaline going for those athletes involved. Here are some explanations, excuses, and alibis for the fear factor.

... ...

Running back Preston Pearson of the Dallas Cowboys, on why he opted for basketball over football during his college days at the University of Illinois:

"I was scared. We had guys like Dick Butkus walking around campus."

...

Former major-league shortstop Gene Michael, regarded as master of the hidden-ball trick, on why he only pulled the trick five times:

"I could have done it more, but I was afraid somebody would beat me up."

...

Roy Danforth, Tulane basketball coach, on why the visiting Green Wave got out of Philadelphia so fast after losing to Penn:

"We were afraid we'd get arrested for impersonating a basketball team."

...

Michigan football coach Bo Schembechler, on his lack of interest in a professional coaching position:

"I'd always fear coaching someone who's more important than I am."

...

Base-stealer Maury Wills, on his rare attempts to steal home:

"Frank Howard used to say that if I tried anything funny like stealing home when he was up, he'd take my head off with his bat."

...

Chicago Bears safety Doug Plank, on why he failed to tackle Miami Dolphins fullback Larry Csonka:

"I was trying to tackle him around the ankles, but he was carrying so many of our men, I was afraid I'd hit a teammate."

...

Former champion race-car driver Jackie Stewart on why he was declining a chance to take a ride down the bobsled/luge course at the Winter Olympics:

"It looks a bit too dangerous for me."

...

Safety Mike Wagner, on how the two-time defending Super Bowl champion Pittsburgh Steelers won six consecutive games after dropping four of their first five during the 1976 season:

"It's simple. Jack Lambert got up in the locker room and said if we lost another game, he'd kill every one of us."

...

Former Houston Astro Bob Watson, on the reason he avoided facing Houston fastballer J. R. Richard in batting practice:

"I have a family to think about."

...

Lee Corso, Indiana football coach, on why the team wasn't partaking of a fruitcake sent by an anonymous fan:

"All of us would like to eat it, but we're scared. When you're 2–8, you don't mess around with any unsigned fruitcakes."

...

Gene Mauch, Minnesota Twins manager, on why he let starting pitcher Pete Redfern struggle for more than four innings before taking him out for a reliever:

"I was afraid I might strangle him if I had him in the dugout."

...

Tom Casanova, Cincinnati Bengals safety, and his alibi for not playing on the kickoff-return team:

"Basically, I'm scared."

...

Cincinnati relief pitcher Clay Carroll, on how he suffered a bruised collarbone during a fight between the Reds and the Los Angeles Dodgers:

"We were trying to get the bullpen gate open. We couldn't get it open, and then it flew back and hit me. I got punched out by a gate."

...

New York Rangers center Rod Gilbert, excusing himself for punching Bill Lesuk of the Philadelphia Flyers during a National Hockey League (NHL) contest:

"He hit me on the head with his stick. And he didn't apologize."

...

Seattle SuperSonics forward Xavier McDaniel, gave this alibi for getting into a fight with 7' center Kevin Willis of the Atlanta Hawks:

"I thought he was going to hit me first, so I hit him first."

...

When Steve Garvey of the Los Angeles Dodgers scored on a hard slide at the plate following his 1,999th career hit, an angry St. Louis Cardinals catcher Darrell Porter explained why he followed Garvey into the Dodger dugout:

"I thought it was his 2,000th hit and I wanted to go over and congratulate him."

...

Hall of Fame offensive tackle Roosevelt Brown, one of the least penalized players in the game, on the reason he had been called for an unnecessary-roughness penalty:

"It wasn't my fault. It all started when he hit me back."

...

Oakland manager Billy Martin, who, after an upsetting performance by the A's hit a piece of furniture and broke his finger:

"I'm getting smarter. I finally punched something that couldn't sue me."

...

Bob Ferry, former Baltimore Bullet center, explaining his version of a scuffle with Wilt Chamberlain of the Philadelphia 76ers:

"I threw a left hook, but I was backpedaling so fast it never got there."

...

Hall of Fame shortstop Rabbit Maranville once picked a fight with a cabbie and lost. When he fought three more cabbies and lost each time, he explained to team owner Bill Veeck:

"I'm trying to find one I can whip."

...

New York Rangers defenseman Barry Beck, on the culprit responsible for a bench-clearing brawl with the Los Angeles Kings:

"We have only one person to blame and that's each other."

...

Pittsburgh Pirates pitcher Bob Walk, who came off the bench excusing himself for jumping on top of a pile of players during a brawl with Montreal:

"I was kind of practicing for winning the World Series."

...

Former professional football player Alex Hawkins, telling an Atlanta Falcons player why he refused to go outside a bar to fight:

"Oh, no, not until you sober up. If I hit you now it wouldn't hurt."

...

Oakland A's slugger Mark McGwire, on the reason he avoids ending up on the bottom of the pile during baseball extracurricular activities:

"You can't do anything and you're eating grass the whole time."

...

Clay Carroll, Cincinnati Reds reliever, on his decision to leave the safety of the bullpen and go to the mound to join in a player brawl:

"I thought maybe I'd pick up another save."

9
Mind Games

MEMORY LANE

"I don't recollect." "I don't recall." "I don't remember." These sayings were the most popular excuses used by those witnesses testifying at the Watergate scandal hearings in the 1970s. How convenient! Sports figures also have their share of memory lapses, which prove to be somewhat more legitimate as excuses.

... ...

When Oklahoma was recruiting Mickey Mantle for football, he was shown around by Sooners quarterback Darrell Royal. Years later, they met again on the sidelines during a game between the Royal-coached Texas Longhorns and TCU. Mantle recalled their earlier meeting. But Royal didn't, and Mantle reported that the coach offered this excuse:

"He said, 'Hell, I don't remember. You weren't Mickey Mantle then.' "

...

Heavyweight champion Jack Dempsey, hit by a solid right in the first round, later explaining to his wife, Estelle, why he lost a 10-round decision and the title to Gene Tunney:

"Honey, I just forgot to duck."

...

Jack Nicklaus, on why he couldn't recall the golfing tips he offered to former president Gerald Ford during a practice round:

"There were so many of them."

...

Bill Lewis, Wyoming football coach, after the Cowboys were demolished 45–0 by Arizona State:

"We felt we had a good week of practice. We just forgot how to play."

...

Boxer Ken Norton had a good excuse for not remembering anything about being kayoed by Gerry Cooney just 54 seconds into round one:

"I guess I was unconscious."

...

Rocky Bridges, former major leaguer, longtime coach, and minor-league manager, recalling a pitcher's alibi for missing a sign to swing away after failing on a bunt attempt:

"Well, I forgot."

MENTAL GYMNASTICS

Someone once remarked that 90 percent of sports is mental. If that's true, some athletes are in big trouble! Both players and coaches, however, are smart enough to produce excuses and explanations based on the intellectual side of sports.

... ...

San Diego Padres catcher Bruce Bochy offered this excuse after he was thrown out on one of his rare steal attempts:

"As I was running down to second, a lot of things were going through my mind."

...

Tom Watson, explaining his disqualification for illegally changing putters during a PGA tournament round delayed by rain:

"My IQ must be two points lower than a plant's."

...

Gene Murphy, Cal State–Fullerton football coach, on the reason his team made so many mistakes in losing the California Bowl 20–17 to Northern Illinois:

"We have some people out there who need lobotomies between terms."

...

Jockey Steve Cauthen, who rode Triple Crown winner Affirmed, when asked how he psyches up for a race:

"I don't psyche myself up. I psyche myself down. I think clearer when I'm not psyched up."

Dallas Cowboys halfback Duane Thomas, on whether he had an IQ:

"Sure I've got one. It's a perfect 20–20."

...

Bill Fitch, Cleveland Cavaliers coach, on why he put on a referee's warmup jacket after getting a technical foul:

"I plead temporary insanity."

...

Casey Stengel, explaining the mental impact of his football career:

"I played football before they had headgear and that's how I lost my mind."

...

Pro tennis player Johan Kriek, after suffering a first-round upset loss during a tournament played on a slow, clay surface:

"I don't know why the hell I enter this tournament ... I don't have the mental capacity to stay out there for four hours and hit junk."

...

New York running back Clark Gaines, on the Jets' 20–10 loss to the Buffalo Bills:

"We moved from the 20 to 20, but we made mental mistakes. That's something the game plan doesn't allow for."

...

Seattle coach Bill Russell, after his players abandoned the game plan, on why the SuperSonics went on to lose to the Boston Celtics:

"We lost it above the shoulders."

...

Lineman Steve Tannen of the New York Jets, explaining his mental preparation:

"Some people have trouble getting 'up' for a game. I get so high I have to get 'down.' So I write poetry."

...

Golf pro Bobby Nichols, on his mental game:

"If you have to remind yourself to concentrate, you have no chance to concentrate."

...

Joe Thomas, Baltimore general manager and coach, on why the Colts defeated the New York Jets:

"You can't win when you have to think so I cut the game plan drastically."

...

Milwaukee Brewer outfielder Jim Wohlford, explaining the mental side of baseball:

"Ninety percent of this game is half mental."

BACK TO THE DRAWING BOARD

Ah, the best laid plans of mice and men! Nobody ever claimed that every strategy or tactic would always work perfectly. Failure means it's time to go back to the drawing board! When tactics do work, what the strategy was and what is actually claimed as brilliant strategy by coaches are most likely to be two entirely different things.

... ...

Arkansas football coach Lou Holtz, explaining the meticulous strategy behind the Razorbacks' triple option offense:

"One back carries the ball, one back fumbles it, and the third one is supposed to recover it."

...

USC basketball coach Stan Morrison, in the pre-shot-clock era, on the reason his team didn't use a four-corner offense to stall late in the game:

"The problem is that all our players wind up in one corner."

...

Ed Doherty, former Xavier University football coach, on why he once told his quarterback to take a safety with seconds left in the game even though his team had the ball at midfield and was leading Marshall, 3–0:

"I always wanted to be in a 3–2 game."

...

Kansas City Kings coach Phil Johnson thought his
diagrammed inbounds play had produced a last-
second basket to defeat the Houston Rockets. The only
problem was that guard Larry Drew stepped on the
out-of-bounds line during his throw-in. Explained
Johnson:

> *"I designed the play without realizing what big
> feet Larry had. I should have moved him over
> six inches in my diagram."*

...

Ed Murphy, University of Mississippi basketball coach, explaining his time-out with two minutes left in a game that Florida led by 20 points:

"The last time-out was to take the sandwich orders."

...

Russell "Sox" Walseth, University of Colorado basketball coach, on why he called back-to-back time-outs without letting play resume in a game against Missouri:

"During the first time-out I got everybody on my team so thoroughly confused I had to call another one right away to straighten things out."

...

Oklahoma City University basketball coach Abe Lemons, on the reason his strategy is to keep his plays simple:

"You could tell five guys to go over to the post office at 2 o'clock and one of 'em wouldn't be there. So why have so many tricky plays?"

...

Richie Adubato, Dallas Mavericks assistant coach and clipboard strategist, analyzing a chair-throwing brawl on the Geraldo Rivera show that resulted in a broken nose for the host:

"It didn't look like he got any weakside help."

...

Male wrestler Lynn Martin, on why he chose to default a 115-pound match against female wrestler Rhonda Bingham of Bellevue (Washington) High School:

"You couldn't use half your moves."

10
Relationships

LOVE AND KISSES

Falling in love can sometimes turn the fine line between sports success or failure into a brick wall. Before love blossoms, the kissing game must be explored. Sometimes, kissing is more complicated than love. Here are some romantic excuses from the world of love and kisses.

... ...

Randy Neil, founder of the International Cheerleading Foundation, on the reason the organization took so long to achieve success:

> *"For the first few years, I was falling in love every other month."*

...

Los Angeles Dodgers outfielder Mickey Hatcher, on why he opted not to give Kirk Gibson a big smooch after Gibson's dramatic, ninth-inning home run beat Oakland in Game 1 of the 1988 World Series:

> *"I wanted to go out and kiss the guy, but he never shaves."*

Detroit Tigers outfielder Kirk Gibson, on his excuse for striking out while actress Morgan Fairchild—whom he was reportedly dating—was looking on from the stands:

"I kept looking at her instead of the ball."

...

Morganna Roberts, alias the "Kissing Bandit," on her alibi for kissing Seattle Mariners catcher Steve Yeager on the cheek instead of the lips:

"I think he chews tobacco."

...

Charlie Simmer of the Los Angeles Kings, explaining his five-game scoreless slump after making wedding plans following his engagement to Terry Welles, a *Playboy* magazine playmate of the month:

"That's why I was in a slump, thinking about all that new responsibility."

...

Jeannette Baldwin, after her husband Ralph Baldwin piloted Speedy Scot to victory in the famed Hambletonian, on why she didn't give the horse a congratulatory kiss:

"I would have kissed him—but he bites.'

THAT'S NO LADY, THAT'S MY WIFE!

What better person for a husband to use to justify or excuse his behavior than his wife? Indeed, wives provide their husbands with fertile grounds for excuses and explanations. These may involve such things as money matters, raising children, and spending time together.

> ᵗ

... ...

Ted Giannoulas, otherwise known as the San Diego Chicken, on why he hadn't gotten married yet:

"I don't think any wife would stand for a husband traveling around dressed like a chicken."

...

Thoroughbred trainer Horatio Luro—noting that he could give the female owners who hired him his excuses for racing losses during short phone conversations—on the reason he refused to train his wife's horses:

"For your wife, you can go home to make the excuses. Maybe the conversation never ends."

...

Former middleweight boxing champion Jake LaMotta, explaining why his first of six wives left him:

"I clashed with the drapes."

...

Ray Perkins, head coach of the New York Giants, on whether his wife disapproves of his 18-hour workdays:

"I don't know. I don't see her that much."

...

Mrs. Bob Tyler, spouse of Mississippi State coach Bob Tyler, explaining the life of a football coach's wife:

"It's like being the copilot to a kamikaze pilot."

Pro tennis player Johan Kriek, on his explanation for returning to play in the French Open after skipping the event the previous seven years:

"My wife wanted to do some shopping in Paris."

...

Miami Dolphins coach Don Shula, on his excuse for not selecting his son, Dave, a Dartmouth wide receiver, in the NFL draft:

"Because my wife would have insisted that the quarterback throw to him on every play."

...

Iowa football coach Bob Commings, a guard during his playing days, on why his son became a quarterback:

"My mother raised some dummies, but not my wife."

...

Cincinnati Bengals coach Forrest Gregg, on the reason he allowed his players' wives to spend the evening with their husbands the night before the 1982 Super Bowl:

"Because they're married to them."

...

Tennis player Ilie Nastase, on why he failed to report that his American Express Card had been stolen:

"Whoever stole it is spending less money than my wife."

THE FAIR SEX

Ever notice how men blame women and women blame men? Those doing the blaming will state with frustration, "All men (women) are alike." Here are some quotes where men attribute their failures or decisions to *guess who*?

... ...

Detroit coach Bob Kauffman, on the cause of the Pistons' terrible 2–27 road record against West Coast teams during the previous season:

"All the distracting broads."

...

Boston Red Sox manager Ralph Houk, on his motivation for coming back to managing and leaving his Florida golf game behind:

"Women were outdriving me."

...

Former professional boxer Willie Pep, explaining his failure to become a millionaire:

"I just got things reversed. My women were too fast and my horses too slow."

...

Bill van Breda Kolff, on why he took the head coaching position at the University of New Orleans after once vowing he would never coach college basketball again:

"Women aren't the only ones who can change their minds."

GOOD OL' MOM

Dad often gets the credit for an athlete's success but good ol' mom plays a key role, too. Moms provide encouragement and support to help their children be the best they can be as athletes and as persons. They also sometimes receive criticism or praise for their role. Here are some insightful "mom" quotes.

... ...

Arnold Palmer, explaining how he got his famous hitch:

"I've always had narrow hips and when I was a kid, my pants were always sliding down. My mother was always saying, 'Arnold, pull up your pants.' I started pulling them up to please Mom."

...

Alabama football coach Bear Bryant, on why he didn't wear his familiar houndstooth hat for the Sugar Bowl game at the Louisiana Superdome:

"My mother told me never to wear a hat indoors."

...

Bill Riordan, former business manager for Jimmy Connors, blaming the tennis pro's mother for Connors' early-round Wimbledon loss to Roscoe Tanner in 1976:

"I think there's a time to leave the nest and I think that time has come."

...

Cincinnati Reds pitcher Jack Billingham, one of the worst hitters in the major leagues, on how he hit .450 batting cleanup for his high school team:

"My mother was the official scorer."

COACHES AND PLAYERS

Face it, coaches and players are seldom on the same wavelength. The relationship is almost always adversarial. Coaches want too much discipline; players want too little. Do coaches and players really get to know each other? Both, however, are good at coming up with explanations.

... ...

Famed knuckleball pitcher Hoyt Wilhelm, after retiring as a hurler at age 49, explaining his new role as a minor-league manager:

"Now I'll see if I can control a few knuckleheads."

...

Iowa football coach Bob Commings, on the reason for the Hawkeyes' 38–14 loss to Purdue:

"After looking at the films, I would say that none of our players did poorly individually. But collectively we were lousy."

...

University of Texas basketball coach Abe Lemons, explaining why he avoids player substitutions when his team is losing:

"I don't want some turkey to look good and then have to play him the next five games."

Walt Garrison, former Dallas fullback, on whether Cowboys coach Tom Landry ever smiles:

"I don't know, I only played there nine years."

...

Dick Buechler, Xavier University tackle, explaining why the team went 6–4 under first-year coach Ed Biles:

"We would have presented Coach Biles with an undefeated season, but we didn't think he was ready for it."

JUST LOVE THOSE ALUMS

Ah, college sports. Perhaps the most fickle relationship is that between coach and the diehard alums of Whatsamatta U. When their team is winning, coaches manage to tolerate the alumni. When their team is losing, alumni don't tolerate coaches for very long. Here are some quotes from coaches regarding this sometimes tenuous relationship.

... ...

Florida State football coach Bobby Bowden, explaining why he passed up an alumni fishing trip:

"After losing to Florida the way we did last year it might not be a good idea for me to get out on a boat with some of our alumni."

...

Lou Holtz, Minnesota Gophers football coach, on his excuse for always pacing the sidelines:

"A moving target is harder to hit."

...

Gene Stallings, Dallas Cowboys assistant coach, on the reason he didn't pay much attention to alumni during his days as a college head coach:

"If you listen to them, you wind up sitting with them in the stands."

...

Phil Cutchin, former Oklahoma State football coach, on why he retired to raise cattle:

"Cattle have no alumni."

ATHLETIC SUPPORTERS

What would teams do without their athletic supporters? Since jocks, coaches, and owners are all impacted by good or poor fan support, this results in excuses. Sometimes they even make excuses for the fans! Here are some quotes regarding the fan.

... ...

Owner Jack Kent Cooke, on the reason for the Los Angeles Kings' low attendance figures in the early 1970s:

"There are 800,000 Canadians living in the Los Angeles area, and I've just discovered why they left Canada. They hate hockey."

...

Kansas City Royals owner Ewing Kauffman, explaining to Washington, D.C., media why the city doesn't have a major-league baseball franchise:

"You don't have a core there to support it, a core of industry that will buy tickets. You've got a lot of U.S. government workers and all they do is ask for free tickets."

Larry Lacewell, Arkansas State football coach, on why he does his coaching from the press box and not from the sidelines:

> *"Our coaching staff likes it because I'm out of their way. Also the boos aren't quite so loud."*

...

The Cincinnati Reds' Pete Rose, explaining a benefit of his position switch from left field to third base:

> *"You meet a better class of fan around third base."*

...

In the days before Magic Johnson and NBA titles for the Los Angeles Lakers, Kareem Abdul-Jabbar explained the team's failure to sell out home games:

> *"When it's the middle of January and the sun is shining and it's beautiful outside, who wants to come in and see the Lakers lose?"*

...

Chicago coach Abe Gibron, on the reason the Bears no longer had three kicking specialists on their roster:

> *"We can't afford to have so many spectators on the sidelines."*

ANIMAL LOVERS

Some people love their pets so much they do rather bizarre things—such as treating their animals as humans. Sports figures are no exception. Here are some explanations and excuses involving pets.

New York Mets infielder Doug Flynn on why Woody,
his sheepdog, flew first class to Florida:

"Because he likes champagne."

...

Boxer Alfredo Escalera, on whether he had experienced any problems in airports because his traveling companion is a python:

"No, he has a passport."

...

Don Cherry, Boston Bruins coach, on the reason he calls his players dogs:

"There's no higher compliment in the world that I can pay another human being—because I love dogs, more than I do most human beings."

...

When Indiana coach Bobby Knight missed the Big Ten Conference's annual preseason media function, Michigan State coach Jud Heathcote offered this excuse for Knight's absence:

"There was a death in the family. His dog died."

11
The Art of Communication

IT'S ALL GREEK TO ME

Athletes are not exactly linguists. But they do seem to understand plain English, dirty language, slang, body language, and the jargon of their particular sport. Here are some examples of both their understanding and mastery of language and their lack of language abilities.

... ...

Hubert "Geese" Ausbie of the Harlem Globetrotters, explaining to China Deputy Premier Teng Hsiao-ping why he mispronounced his name:

"Mr. Premier, we are expert at bouncin', *not* pronouncin'."

...

Casey Stengel, on the reason he never visited Montreal:

"Because then there'd be two languages I couldn't speak—French and English."

Hockey great Gordie Howe, on the language abilities of professional athletes:

"All pro athletes are bilingual. They speak English and profanity."

...

Uwe Blab, Indiana center and West German native, explaining to coach Bobby Knight why he couldn't give him some German swear words to use with officials:

"Then you'd know what I was saying to you."

...

Teenage quarter-miler Robin Campbell—a winner in a US–USSR indoor meet—on the difference between Americans and Russians:

"You can't understand what the Russians say."

...

Argentine golf pro Roberto de Vicenzo, explaining his flawed English:

"I learn English from American professionals, especially Jim Turnesa, that's why I speak so bad. I call it PGA English."

...

Duke basketball coach Mike Krzyzewski—complimenting Navy players for using three-syllable words and full sentences during a pregame press conference—on his own language deficiencies:

"I'm only up to two syllables, but I'm Polish so I have an excuse."

...

Glenn Sheeley, pro football writer for an Atlanta newspaper, explaining his coverage of the NFL's preseason:

"Following the lead of NFL coaches who do not play many of their starters, I don't use any of my first-string verbs and adjectives."

...

Arkansas football coach Lou Holtz, on the reason he prohibits swearing during team practices:

"The Lord allows only so much profanity per team . . . and I use up our entire quota."

...

Seve Ballesteros, explaining why he and Lee Trevino didn't converse in Spanish during a practice round:

"Trevino speaks Mexican."

SAY WHAT?

Don't they say the strangest things! It's easy to do a doubletake upon perusing these examples of some slightly confused and misstated explanations. They know what they meant to say, right?

... ...

Former president Gerald Ford, on his sports viewing habits:

"I watch a lot of baseball on radio."

...

Jim Gantner, Milwaukee Brewers infielder, on the reason he forgot to make a scheduled appearance on a radio show:

"I must have had ambrosia."

...

Kansas City Royals relief pitcher Dan Quisenberry, explaining his control problems:

"I found a delivery in my flaw."

...

Philadelphia manager Danny Ozark, on why the Phillies weren't suffering a morale problem after fading from the pennant race:

"Morality at this time isn't a factor."

...

Frank Burns, Rutgers football coach, on whether his team still aspired to a bowl game after a late-season loss:

"I've only heard what I read in the papers."

...

Georgia basketball coach Hugh Durham, explaining his philosophy of the game:

"It's not how good you can play when you play good. It's how good you play when you play bad and we can play bad as good as anyone in the country."

LOOK WHO'S TALKING!

Some people in athletics can talk a good game, others can back up their talk, and still others don't want to talk at all. To each his own! With all the talkers—and nontalkers—an abundance of excuses and explanations exists for both free speech and no speech.

... ...

Muhammad Ali, on why his slurred speech was becoming more difficult to understand:

"If you talked as much as I do, your voice would be tired, too."

...

Duane Thomas, on the reason he very rarely talked to the media during his days as a running back for the Dallas Cowboys:

"It's not that I wouldn't talk. It was that I wasn't really prepared to talk."

...

New York Islanders goalie Chico Resch, explaining why he is such a prolific talker:

"If I wasn't talking, I wouldn't know what to say."

...

New York Mets slugger Dave Kingman—after belting a pair of three-run homers—telling reporters why he was refusing postgame interviews:

"I've got better things to do than talk with you guys."

...

107

Portland Trail Blazers center Bill Walton, explaining his decision to stop speaking out on controversial political issues:

"I've learned that there's a time when it's in the team's interest not to say anything and in some instances not saying anything is really saying a lot. A lot of people understand what not saying anything means, so, in effect, not saying anything is really saying a lot."

...

Boxer Archie Moore, on why he accepts speaking engagements at prisons:

"Because nobody walks out in the middle of my speech."

...

LeRoy Irvin, Kansas defensive back, on the reason he enjoys yapping to the receivers he covers:

"I just want them to know who's robbin' the train."

...

Philadelphia Phillies manager Danny Ozark, trying to explain how much infielder Bill Grabarkewitz talks:

"Bill talks so much that if you could attach a watch to his jaw you'd never have to wind it."

...

Florida football coach Charley Pell—called at home by a reporter the night before announcing his resignation—on why he wouldn't comment about resignation rumors:

"I hadn't intended to talk to any press tonight. I only answered the phone because I thought my wife was in the bathroom."

...

Muhammad Ali, explaining that his hysterical verbal profession of "I'm the Greatest" was just a put-on:

"I just said I was the greatest. I never thought I was."

LOCKER-ROOM PEP

Notre Dame football coach Knute Rockne's "Win one for the Gipper" is perhaps the most famous pep talk of all time. It worked, after all! Of course, coaches and players don't normally discuss the pep talks that failed to bring a victory. So, the pep-talk reviews are mixed. But they still may serve as an excuse or explanation for winning or losing.

... ...

Tampa Bay coach John McKay, explaining the outcome of his speech before the Buccaneers' 34–0 loss to the New York Jets:

"I told the players to go out and have some fun, and they took me literally."

...

Cleveland coach Bill Fitch, on the reason for the Cavaliers' come-from-behind triumph over the Buffalo Braves on Christmas:

"We got in the Christmas spirit in the first half. At halftime I said, 'Bah, humbug.'"

...

Larry Lacewell, Oklahoma defensive coach, on the Sooners' second-half defensive improvement against Florida State:

"I told them at the half, if they saw a guy carrying the ball to try and tackle him."

WHAT'S IN A NAME?

Wouldn't it have been great to be a pioneer of the Old West? Why? Because these rugged individualists got to name things! Okay, I dub this Lake Louise; that'll be Pikes—no—Fred's Peak; and we'll call this Smithtown! Today, the same spirit exists, with the creation of product and business names, nicknames, and the option to use a middle name instead of a first name. Of course, names can throw curves or make it difficult sometimes, too. But names do make for some great excuses and explanations!

... ...

Boston Celtics star John Havlicek, on the reason the Ralston Cereal Company wanted him for their commercials:

"Then they'd have Wheat Chex, Corn Chex, and Havli-Chex."

...

Pro golfer Kermit Zarley, on why he goes by Kermit instead of his middle name:

"Because my middle name is Millard."

...

Professional golfer J. C. Snead, explaining why he no longer was going by his middle name Carlyle:

"Simple. Carlyle wasn't playing worth a damn."

Niagara University basketball player David Cox from Trumbull, Connecticut, on why he dubbed himself "The Connecticut Yankee":

"Coach is the yanker; I'm the yankee."

...

New York Mets relief pitcher Bob Miller, on his motivation for changing his name from Gmeinweiser:

"I couldn't pronounce it myself."

...

UCLA sports information director Vic Kelly, explaining how to pronounce the name of Bruin linebacker Frank Manumaleuma:

"It's very easy, if you work on it for about a week."

...

Pan American basketball coach Abe Lemons, on why the fact that Texas Rangers manager Billy Martin had made *Who's Who* didn't bother him:

"I remember the time I made Who's That. *"*

...

Joe Frasson, veteran stock-car driver, on why he named his Spartanburg, South Carolina, dinner club the "Excuse Lounge":

"I figured if the lounge made me a bundle of money I would have a good excuse to quit racing."

...

Cleveland Indians manager Jeff Torborg, on the reason his nickname was "The Judge" when he was a catcher with the Los Angeles Dodgers:

"Because I was always sitting on the bench."

...

Light heavyweight James Scott—a New Jersey inmate allowed to box on prison grounds—on his loss to James "The Bull" Martin, whom he had never seen before the bout:

"He has the nickname 'The Bull' and I expected him to be short and stocky. He wasn't. He was lanky, like me. We prepared for a short guy. It threw me off."

...

Tampa Bay Buccaneers coach John McKay, on the reason his "special" teams would now be called "kicking" teams:

"There's nothing special about them. Ours have been unspecial."

...

Southern Methodist University (SMU) point guard Butch Moore, telling coach Dave Bliss why he tabbed him with the nickname "Stevie," after singer Stevie Wonder:

"Coach, with the way you dress, you must be blind."

...

LSU basketball coach Dale Brown, explaining his squad's less-than-energetic, two-point victory over Alabama:

"We are not the LSU Tigers—we're the LSU Somnambulists."

...

Former Boston pitcher Ferguson Jenkins, on why he called Red Sox manager Don Zimmer a buffalo:

"Of all the animals on earth, the buffalo is the dumbest."

...

Former Oakland A's owner Charlie Finley, on why he was revising his prior moniker for baseball commissioner Bowie Kuhn:

"I have often called him the village idiot. I apologize to all the village idiots of America. He's the nation's idiot."

...

San Antonio Spurs guard Mike Dunleavy, on the reason he nicknamed tough Phoenix Suns forward Maurice Lucas "Bogey," after Humphrey Bogart:

"Because Maurice treats all of us like Bogart treated his women—with the back of his hand."

...

The Portland Trail Blazers' Mychal Thompson, on why he dubbed newly signed, stocky rookie Kelvin Ransey "Mrs. Butterworth":

"Because he's thick and rich like the syrup."

...

Dallas Cowboys defensive back Charlie Waters, on the reason his hard-hitting secondary partner Aaron Mitchell was called "A.M.–P.M.":

"Because they're wide awake when he hits 'em and their lights are out when he walks away."

12
The Learning Curve

THE EDUCATIONAL PROCESS

Education doesn't end with formal schooling. It's actually a lifetime process. Of course, this makes for a lifetime of explanations encompassing grade school, high school, college, graduate school, vocational study, and extracurricular activities.

... ...

Hall of Fame pitcher Dizzy Dean, on why his academic life ended after the third grade:

"I only went to the third grade because my father only went to the fourth and I didn't want to pass him."

...

Tennis player Mareen "Peanut" Louie, on why she decided to turn professional at age 18:

"I hate homework."

...

Bob Kuechenberg, Miami Dolphins guard, on his motivation for attending college:

"My father was a human cannonball who used to go around country fairs and rodeos being shot out of a cannon. He used to say, 'Go to college or be a cannonball.'"

...

New York Yankee outfielder Claudell Washington, on his excuse for running track instead of playing baseball in high school:

"Because the track coach was the biology teacher and I had trouble with biology."

...

Texas A&M basketball coach Shelby Metcalf, explaining why a player left the squad:

"He came here when he heard A&M was an engineering school. But when he found out they wouldn't let him drive a train he quit."

...

Quarterback Jim McMahon, on why he wouldn't be graduating from Brigham Young University following his senior season:

"I kinda screwed up my redshirt year, then had to take incompletes in summer school because I went golfing every day."

...

Philadelphia 76ers star Charles Barkley, explaining why he planned to return to Auburn University to earn credits toward a degree despite earning $2 million a year:

"Because my grandma said I have to."

...

Boston Celtics forward Marvin Barnes, on why he made up so many college credits while serving a prison sentence:

"There was no place I could go to cut classes."

...

An anonymous Ohio State football player, explaining to head coach Woody Hayes why he had received four Fs and one D in school:

"I guess I spent too much time on that one subject."

...

Oklahoma coach Barry Switzer, on the reason one of his players had left the university:

"It was like a heart transplant. We tried to implant college in him, but his head rejected it."

...

Former NFL player Alex Karras, with his alibi for never receiving his degree from the University of Iowa:

"I never graduated from Iowa, but I was only there for two terms—Truman's and Eisenhower's."

...

Marquette coach Al McGuire, on his excuse for starting forward Bill Neary—who was averaging only 1.8 points per game:

"I wanted to bring up the grade-point average of the team. Neary's a 3.7. That gives us about a C-minus."

...

Gale Catlett, University of Cincinnati basketball coach, explaining why his team's Garry Kamstra had a bad night in an NCAA tourney regional contest:

> *"He had his nose in a book the whole day and he had a bad game. You can't study all day long and expect to do well later on the basketball court."*

...

Karl Kremser, former Miami Dolphins placekicker, on why he quit as Davidson College soccer coach:

> *"I thought the school had a commitment to soccer, but that wasn't the case . . . its emphasis was on academics."*

...

Rice football coach Al Conover, explaining his schooling:

> *"I have a good educational background. I even have a master's degree. The subject of my thesis was, 'What College Done For Me.'"*

...

George Foreman, on why his educational life would have been different if he didn't have a habit of sleeping in very, very late:

> *"If school had started at 4 o'clock in the afternoon, I would have been a college graduate."*

...

Maurice Spencer, hard-hitting defensive back for the Atlanta Falcons, on why he was pursuing studies toward a future career as a dentist:

"If you've knocked out a few teeth, you owe it to yourself to put a few back in."

...

When Oakland Raiders wide receiver Bob Chandler was getting ready for his team's 1981 Super Bowl appearance, he tried to use that as an excuse for missing the first few classes of his law school studies. "I'll be late on account of the Super Bowl," Chandler told his professor. But his law professor offered his own excuse for not letting Chandler off:

"What's the Super Bowl?"

...

Minnesota signal-caller Fran Tarkenton, on the reason he wasn't interested in training All-America quarterback Tommy Kramer, the Vikings' top draft choice:

"That ain't my job. I don't train quarterbacks."

...

San Diego Padres first baseman Steve Garvey, on why he reads *Playboy* magazine for its educational value:

"I'm trying to be the best possible person I can, using whatever resources it takes. It keeps my focus from being too narrow and allows me to expand and grow with the times."

...

Running back John Riggins, on his toughest transition from college ball at Kansas to the NFL and the New York Jets:

"Learning to drive in New York City."

...

Philadelphia Phillie Dick Allen, on his decision not to tag up from third on a fly ball to Cincinnati Reds centerfielder Cesar Geronimo:

"If I had tried, the way Cesar Geronimo throws, then me and [catcher] Johnny Bench would've had to do a little tangoing at home plate . . . and neither of us has ever gone to any Arthur Murray schools."

...

Longtime New York Mets broadcaster Lindsey Nelson, explaining the three things he had learned in his career:

"Never play poker with a man named Ace, never eat at a place called Mom's, and never invest in anything that eats or needs painting."

GEOGRAPHY LESSONS

Geography never was a strong subject for many people. Today, our youth seem to know even less of the subject. Some sports figures, however, have enough geographical knowledge to use it in their explanations.

... ...

Al Antak, Camas (Washington) High School assistant football coach, explaining his solution after his team's punt-returner ran 54 yards the wrong way for a safety in a 2–0 loss to Prairie High:

"We need to start teaching geography a few years earlier."

...

Mario Andretti—who had to make the long trip to Europe every two weeks to compete on the Grand Prix circuit—on why that's the way it had to be:

"I guess you can't have the French Grand Prix in Milwaukee."

...

New Jersey Devils goalie Chico Resch, explaining the location of his hometown of Moose Jaw, Saskatchewan:

"Four feet away from the moose's butt."

...

Milwaukee Brewers general manager Harry Dalton, on his preference for Arizona as a spring-training site:

"Florida is for old people and their parents."

...

East German Olympic Committee President Manfred Ewald, explaining to an Italian reporter when his country would expand its Winter Olympics participation to Alpine skiing events:

"As soon as you surrender some of your mountains to us."

...

Kansas City Kings rookie Glenn Hansen, on the reason he and the New York Knicks' Phil Johnson were the NBA's only North Dakotans:

"Nobody plays basketball in North Dakota."

...

Los Angeles defenseman Terry Harper, on why the Kings were in the midst of a good season:

"We all love living here so much we have to win if we want to stay."

...

Professional golfer Jim Colbert, on his refusal to get excited after destroying par in the opening round of a tournament:

"The slums of Chicago are full of first-round leaders."

...

Al Braverman, fight manager for Chuck Wepner, on a suggestion that opponent Muhammad Ali might protest the use of a foreign substance on Wepner's face to guard against cuts:

"It's not a foreign substance. It comes from the United States."

GRAVITY OF THE SITUATION

Gravity certainly does have some pull in the sports world. Little did Isaac Newton know that his discovery would serve very well as an alibi and explanation for some sports mysteries.

... ...

San Francisco 49ers quarterback John Brodie—who had a million-dollar contract—on why he had to hold the football on field-goal and extra-point attempts:

"Well, if I didn't, it would fall over."

...

Former Boston Red Sox hurler Bill "Spaceman" Lee, explaining Hall of Famer Carl Yastrzemski's longevity in the major leagues:

"He lasted so long because he had a small center of gravity."

...

Golfer Harry Toscano, and his alibi for struggling during the first round of the PGA's Tucson Open:

"I had some bad gravity out there. It's gravity that makes the ball drop in the hole, right? Well, I was hitting the putts beautiful but the ball wasn't dropping."

...

When Morganna Roberts (alias the "Kissing Bandit") ran onto the Astrodome field and kissed Houston Astros pitcher Nolan Ryan and infielder Dickie Thon, trespassing charges were filed. But word spread that Roberts—who claimed measurements of 60–23–39—would assert that the law of gravity made her tumble over the Dome's railing. Spokeswoman Molly Ancelin of the Houston Sports Association, which operates the Astrodome, explained why the charges were dropped:

"We just figured under the advice of Isaac Newton not to fight the law of gravity."

SCIENTIFIC THEORY

And you thought science had no connection to sports. Wrong, Einstein breath! Here are a couple of pointers about the impact of science in the sports world. Read 'em. Maybe you'll learn something!

... ...

Willie Stargell of the Pittsburgh Pirates, explaining how hitting is a matter of geometry:

"They give you a round bat, and they throw a round ball, and they tell you to hit it square."

...

Jack Nicklaus, on why he tees up the ball so high:

"Through years of experience I have found that air offers less resistance than dirt."

...

Chuck Estrada, former Texas Rangers pitching coach, on the team's method of utilizing its bullpen:

"We had a very scientific system of bringing in relief pitchers. We used the first one who answered the phone."

...

New York Governor Hugh Carey, on the scientific explanation for taking four sons out of school for the Yankees' home opener:

"They are learning the mathematical implications of the impact of an object traveling 90 miles an hour as it comes in contact with a moving, three-foot piece of wood called a bat."

...

When outfielder Jesse Barfield was swapped from the
Toronto Blue Jays to the New York Yankees, he was
asked to explain the chemistry on his former team. His
excuse for not doing so:

*"I don't know anything about chemistry. I
flunked that in high school."*

13
Down the
Career Path

CAREER CHOICES

And what do you want to be when you grow up? How often did adults ask you that question when you were a kid? Remember how you changed your answer every week to keep them entertained? How many adults really, really know what they want to do now—and are doing it? Some sports figures offer their explanations for their career decisions.

... ...

Bill White, New York Yankee broadcaster and former major leaguer, on when he first gave serious thought to an announcing career:

"When I hit .211."

...

Indy car driver Pancho Carter, with his alibi for choosing to risk his life racing cars instead of opting for a safer profession:

"I'm too lazy to work and too chicken to steal."

Pitcher Tom Seaver, explaining why he didn't sign with the Los Angeles Dodgers at the start of his career:

"I told them I wanted $50,000 and they told me dental school would be a very good thing for me to pursue."

...

Kansas State quarterback Doug Bogue, on his excuse for switching his major from veterinary medicine to petroleum geology:

"I didn't want any calls at 4:00 A.M. from people saying 'Fifi is throwing up.'"

...

Pitcher Gaylord Perry, explaining why he continued to pitch in the majors even though the was nearing his 42nd birthday:

"I've never been able to find a better summer job."

...

Bert Blyleven, Pittsburgh Pirates pitcher, on why he gave up catching in his youth:

"When I started to throw the ball back to the pitcher harder than he was throwing to me, we changed positions."

...

Kansas City Royals leadoff man Willie Wilson, on his excuse for only walking 22 times during one season:

"If I wanted to walk, I would have become a mailman."

...

Sam Snead, on why he was pondering his retirement from golf:

"The only reason I ever played golf in the first place was so I could afford to hunt and fish."

...

Willie Auchterlonie, on his excuse for retiring from tournament play after winning the British Open:

"Golf seemed a silly thing to do for a living."

DRESS FOR SUCCESS

Now who would ever think that clothes could produce so many excuses in the sports world? I mean, as coaches sometimes say before sending their team out to be slaughtered by some vastly superior, powerhouse opponent, "Boys, they put their pants on one leg at a time just like we do." But clothes do have an impact. Okay, the offense will attend the fashion class today and the defense will go tomorrow. And tuck your shirt-tails in when you go!

... ...

Lee Trevino, on the reason he prefers to skip professional golf tournaments in California early in the year when the weather is cold:

"I can't swing the way I want to with four sweaters and my pajamas and a rain jacket on."

...

When Oakland A's pitcher Dave Stewart went 1–5 in a seven-game stretch after an 8–0 start, he offered this explanation:

"Every year in spring training they make my pants too tight. After a couple of washings, I can't get my leg up, and that's a major part of my mechanics."

...

Minnesota Vikings nose tackle Henry Thomas, on why he had trouble tackling rookie running back Bo Jackson of the Los Angeles Raiders:

"He was no different from any other back, except that his clothes were tight. I couldn't get my hands on him."

...

ABC-TV's Roone Arledge, on the reason Howard Cosell was not part of the network's 1984 Winter Olympics team:

"Howard's not going to like seeing this, but the reason is he doesn't look good in stretch pants."

...

Heisman Trophy winner Johnny Rodgers was hampered by a pulled hamstring during most of one NFL season. But why did he drive to practice in a Rolls-Royce and wear a full-length mink coat on team road trips?:

"I might as well look good if I can't play good."

...

Los Angeles Kings owner Bruce McNall, explaining why the casual style of clothes worn by coach Robbie Ftorek didn't bother him:

"I never saw a shirt and tie win a hockey game."

...

Jan Stephenson, the Ladies' Professional Golf Association's (LPGA) top glamour golfer, on the reason she wears slacks even in hot weather:

"Frankly, I have lousy legs. They're too skinny."

...

Yun Lou, Chinese men's gymnast, trying to justify his score of 9.20 on the pommel horse while other gymnasts were collecting perfect 10s at the 1984 Summer Olympics:

"Suit too big. Grabbed pants instead of pommel."

...

Wisconsin Rapids manager Tom Zimmer, son of Boston Red Sox manager Don, on why he quit the Midwest League team after a pregame session:

"The lights aren't fit to play under, the uniforms don't fit, so I won't let my players play in them."

...

Houston coach Bum Phillips, on why 6'6" 347-pound Angelo Fields—the Oilers' No. 1 draft choice from Michigan State—wasn't wearing boots when introduced at a press conference:

"They don't have enough cows up in Michigan to make his boots."

...

Boston Celtics television announcer John Dennis, explaining why 5'3" Muggsy Bogues of the Charlotte Hornets was sporting low-cut basketball shoes:

"He has to wear low-cuts. The hightops go over his knees."

...

New York Yankee Lou Piniella, after making an out during a batting slump, offered this excuse to the clubhouse man after ripping off his shoes and throwing them onto the field:

"Get me my Adidas—it's these damn shoes' fault I'm not hitting."

...

Joe Frazier, former heavyweight champion, on his motivation for a boxing comeback at age 37:

"The kids need shoes."

...

When the World Series first began to be played at night, Commissioner Bowie Kuhn had this alibi for not wearing a coat during a Series game despite temperatures in the low 40s:

"It wasn't that I was trying to prove anything; I simply don't like to wear a coat. My general practice is not to wear a coat at baseball games, whether they're played in April, August, or October."

...

Earl Campbell, Texas running back and Heisman
Trophy favorite, on why he had six jerseys torn off his
back during a 213-yard rushing effort against SMU:

*"I just thought I'd leave them something to re-
member me by."*

...

University of Cincinnati basketball coach Ed Badger, after ripping off his coat and slam dunking it to the floor:

"I just wanted to show the crowd my tailored shirt."

...

Indiana University football coach Lee Corso, on why he kept wearing his multicolor, quiltlike sports coat:

"It's my interview jacket. No matter what the colors of the school, they're in the coat."

...

Holiday Bowl selection committee member John Reid, gives his alibi for trying to avoid wearing the committee's prized, bright red sports coat in hotel lobbies:

"People keep trying to give me their luggage."

...

Cleveland Indians manager Pat Corrales, on why he often sports a windbreaker in hot weather:

"It keeps me cooler. People don't believe me, but have you ever seen a naked Arab?"

...

Philadelphia 76ers assistant coach Jack McMahon scouted playground players and remembers a player in Chicago who always wore big knee pads:

"I finally asked him why and he said, 'On the playgrounds, that's where I carry my knife.'"

...

Kansas City Royals manager Billy Gardner, excusing himself for not wearing shorts during the hot temperatures of spring training:

"The last time I was in shorts, I was fired. I spent the day on the beach."

...

Oakland A's pitcher Vida Blue, on the reason he did away with his old, tattered and battered, good-luck baseball cap, which gained much media attention:

"I burned the cap because it was getting more ink than me."

...

Tom Paciorek of the Seattle Mariners, on why he didn't receive any commercial endorsements similar to those of Baltimore Orioles pitcher Jim Palmer:

"Because I couldn't get my fanny into the underwear he wears in those commercials."

...

New York Rangers defenseman Barry Beck, explaining his motivation for serving as an underwear model at a fashion show:

"I thought it would be good exposure."

LET GEORGE DO IT

When it comes to politics, most citizens would rather let George (Bush) do it. Heck, some citizens don't even bother to vote, much less run for office. Sports figures have their own reasons for not running. But when athletes do happen to get elected, there may be a good excuse to keep them in office.

Al McGuire, sports broadcaster and former Marquette coach, explaining why reports he might enter politics were false:

"I really don't have any political aspirations. I don't want my family tree traced."

...

Muhammad Ali, on the reason he turned down suggestions that he run for political office:

"If I was a governor or senator, I'd be limited to one state."

...

Stock-car driver Richard Petty, on his excuse for nixing suggestions that he run in the second spot on the North Carolina Republican Governor–Lieutenant Governor ticket:

"I told them I've never run for second place in my life and why should I start now?"

...

Former Buffalo Bills quarterback Jack Kemp, explaining his game plan for getting the citizens of Buffalo to re-elect him to Congress:

"I told people that if they didn't elect me, I'd come back as quarterback of the Bills."

DON'T CALL US,
WE'LL CALL YOU

So much for that job interview! Hiring decisions sometimes are made for peculiar reasons. Of course, the
new hires also must come up with exotic explanations
to justify their new employment status.

... ...

Art Rooney, owner of the Pittsburgh Steelers and
various race horses, on how he picked Chuck Noll as
the team's head coach:

*"His pedigree was super. He was by Paul Brown,
out of Sid Gillman, by Don Shula."*

...

Gene Lamont, Pittsburgh Pirates third-base coach, on
why he wouldn't apply for the vacant manager's job
with the Seattle Mariners:

*"I never heard of anybody getting a job they
applied for."*

...

Oklahoma basketball coach Billy Tubbs, asked upon
his hiring to explain how he felt about being the
school's second choice for the job:

*"It doesn't bother me. I was also my wife's sec-
ond choice, and we've been married 25 years."*

...

Ex-NFL quarterback Joe Kapp, on his hiring as University of California football coach despite no previous coaching experience:

"Howard Cosell coaches 28 NFL teams every week, so I figure I can coach one college team."

GIVE 'EM THE AXE

A tough decision is made. The axe falls heavily. You're fired! Here are some explanations from both sides of the management-employee fence as to why the dreaded axe fell.

... ...

Oakland A's owner Charlie Finley, after axing one of the team's broadcasters:

"He didn't make the games exciting enough when nothing was going on."

...

Billy Tohill, TCU football coach, on the reason he was fired after compiling an 11–15 record:

"I guess it was because I chewed tobacco and cussed a lot."

...

Mike Shure, public relations director of the NBA Buffalo Braves, explaining the termination of coach Jack Ramsay's contract:

"He's not fired. He's just not rehired."

...

Jerry Coleman, on why he didn't ask management the reason he was fired as manager of the San Diego Padres:

"If I did, they might have told me."

...

San Francisco 49ers coach Dick Nolan, on his firing:

"In order to win, everybody has to be on the same page. Naturally, you're going to have problems, in other areas, if everyone's not on the same page."

...

Texas native Bobby Bragan—who had stints as a baseball manager at Pittsburgh, Cleveland, Milwaukee, and Atlanta—on why he always wanted to manage Houston:

"That way, when I got fired I could just drive home."

...

Butler University basketball coach Joe Sexson, explaining how he learned of his imminent "resignation" from newspaper accounts:

"I just saw this in the paper. It appears that I am going to resign this weekend."

...

Kyle Bartee, Lubbock (Texas) Christian College athletic committee member, on why football coach Jerry Don Saunders was let go after registering a 1–18 record:

"You can only take so many of these great lessons in humility."

READY FOR THE ROCKING CHAIR

When does an athlete or coach realize it's time to retire? Such difficult decisions are not helped by large, lucrative contract terms. So the tendency is to hang on longer perhaps than one should. Here are some explanations and excuses on both the pro and con side of the retirement rocking chair.

... ...

George Blanda, 48-year-old Oakland Raiders placekicker, on the reason he wasn't quite ready to retire from pro football after a lengthy career:

"I tried it once in 1959, and I didn't like it."

...

Johnny Kerr, Chicago Bulls broadcaster and ex-NBA center, on why he retired:

"I was driving down the lane one game and the ref called me for three seconds."

...

New York Giants quarterback Y. A. Tittle, on what tipped him off that it was retirement time:

"When the other players started asking me for permission to date my daughter."

...

Former catcher Tom Haller, brother of major league umpire Bill Haller, on what convinced him to end his long career after spending a season with the Detroit Tigers:

"When you have a brother who's an umpire and you're still only hitting .200, it's time to get out."

...

George Halas, on why he finally retired as coach of the Chicago Bears:

"I knew it was time to quit when I was chewing out an official and he walked off the penalty faster than I could keep up with him."

...

Former Boston Celtics center Dave Cowens, on the reason for his retirement:

"I have a highly weakened and worn out set of feet and ankles . . . and it is unbelievably frustrating to remain in a rugged occupation with waning skills."

...

Former Dallas Cowboys defensive back Cornell Green, explaining when a football player realizes it's time to hang up the cleats:

"When he's too tired to make the postgame parties Sunday night."

...

Jim Howell, longtime college basketball official, on his motivation for retiring during basketball season:

"I'm even more tired of going up and down the road than up and down the court."

...

Washington Husky football coach Don James, explaining why rumors of his retirement were just that:

"I've got a daughter that I've got to get through college and I've got a wife who's a world-class shopper."

...

Willie Shoemaker, horse racing's all-time winningest jockey, on the reason he was still riding at the age of 60:

"Who says when you're 60 years old you have to retire and go sit some place and act like an old man?"

14
It's a Business

GET DOWN TO THE
NITTY GRITTY

Sure, money—or lack of it—is usually the excuse for the signing or not signing of a contract with a sports franchise. But sometimes pure greed isn't the only reason contracts are or aren't signed. Included with these financial explanations are some rather outrageous reasons offered for contract decisions.

... ...

Rod Laver, on his excuse for not inking a contract to join the Los Angeles Strings of World Team Tennis:

"They made me an offer I could afford to refuse."

...

New York Yankee owner George Steinbrenner, on why he gave a multimillion dollar contract to Dave Winfield—a former University of Minnesota basketball star—without seeing him play much baseball:

"I never saw anybody tougher off the boards."

Boris Becker, explaining why he wears a watch during his tennis matches:

"Well, I have a contract with the watch company."

...

Casey Merrill, New York Giants defensive end, on the reason he ended his holdout and returned to New York City:

"I didn't want to miss Halloween in New York. Halloween is different in New York than anywhere else."

...

Pitcher Ken Holtzman, on why he hadn't yet agreed to contract terms with the Chicago Cubs:

"We're still about two Cadillacs apart."

...

New York Mets holdout Ed Kranepool, explaining why he didn't take his salary negotiation case to arbitration:

"Arbitration came too late for me. I'm in the twilight of a mediocre career."

...

Cleveland Indians general manager Phil Seghi, on why he signed free-agent pitcher and 20-game winner Wayne Garland:

"If you want to dance, you have to pay the fiddler."

...

McNeese State running back Buford Jordan, explaining why he chose to sign with the USFL's New Orleans Breakers instead of with an NFL team:

"The NFL plays during the holidays and I never liked to play on holidays."

...

Grambling forward Aaron James, on why he signed with the New Orleans Jazz instead of joining the American Basketball Association:

"Because the American Basketball Association is kind of flaky."

...

Tom Grieve, Texas Rangers general manager, on the reason he decided not to make a contract offer to free-agent Bob Horner:

"I read where he was embarrassed by the $4.5 million Atlanta offered. I didn't want to add to his embarrassment."

...

Jerry West, on why he refused an offer from the American Basketball Association and re-signed for the lower figure offered by the Los Angeles Lakers:

"I'd like to believe I have some allegiance to a club that has been awfully nice to me."

AGENT, SMAGENT, I'LL DO IT MYSELF!

What would you do if some professional team wanted to ink you to a lucrative contract? There are good apples and bad apples in the agent biz just as in other occupations. Do you put your trust in an agent or go it alone? These athletes came up with some good explanations for doing it their way.

... ...

Detroit Tigers pitcher Mark "The Bird" Fidrych, on the reason he had no use for an agent:

"Why should I give somebody 10 percent when I do all the work?"

...

Max Montoya, Cincinnati Bengals offensive guard, on why he conducted his contract negotiations without an agent:

"A lot of people have told me I'm crazy for not using an agent, but I think I know my situation better than any agent could. Besides, I'm cheap."

...

Buffalo guard Joe DeLamielleure, explaining why he negotiated his own contract with the Bills:

"There's no need to have an agent if your record speaks for itself. Besides, no lawyer would work for me. They charge by the hour and my talks only took 30 minutes."

IN THE MONEY

Sometimes one might think that Vince Lombardi's words on winning had been changed to "Money isn't everything, it's the only thing!" in the sports world. While the average American worries more about how to pay the bills each month, athletes have other problems. Here are some excuses, alibis, and the explanations that shed light on sports figures' motivations and opinions toward the fiscal world.

... ...

The San Diego Chicken, alias Ted Giannoulas, on why he rejected all movie offers:

"They've offered only a poultry sum."

...

TCU track coach Guy Thompson, recalling the excuse a Horned Frog sprinter gave for his poor performance in a Texas Relays race:

"He told me he didn't think the meal money was sufficient."

...

An out-of-shape Muhammad Ali—after a six-round exhibition late in his career against Jimmy Ellis—on why he wasn't embarrassed to accept a $75,000 paycheck for the effort:

"They came to see Elvis Presley when he was fat and out of shape in his last days."

...

New York coach Dick Howser, on the fast start of Yankee pitcher Doc Medich, who had completed medical school in the off-season:

"He's trying to make enough money to pay the first premium on his malpractice insurance."

...

Rich Kelley, veteran NBA center from Stanford, excusing himself from a Hare Krishna donation request at an airport:

"I gave in another life."

...

When the umpire asked 14-year-old Portland batboy Sam Morris to retrieve a chair tossed on the field by ejected Beaver manager Lee Elia, Morris refused at the urging of Portland players. His excuse for not doing what Pacific Coast League umpire Pam Postema wanted?:

"The Beavers pay me, and I gotta do what they say."

...

Joe Louis, on who hit him the hardest during his boxing career:

"Uncle Sam."

...

Seattle University junior guard Frank Oleynick, explaining how he could declare himself eligible for the NBA draft as a hardship case despite his middle-class background:

"Any time you pass up $100,000 or so, that's a hardship."

...

Forward Mike Green, who played in both the American Basketball Association—which eventually folded—and the National Basketball Association, on the difference between the two leagues:

"In the NBA you get paid."

...

Chris Bahr, placekicker for the Oakland Raiders, on why he switched to football after just a single season with professional soccer's Philadelphia Atoms:

"I got $2,500 for the season in soccer."

...

Ray Floyd, on why he chose LPGA golfer Pat Bradley over his own golfing sister, Marlene, as his partner in the Mixed Team Championship:

"There's a lot of money at stake."

...

World Boxing Council (WBC) heavyweight champion Larry Holmes, explaining why he didn't need to create more action during a sparring session as demanded by some ringside hecklers:

"I don't have to—I'm rich."

...

Lee Trevino, during the prime of his career, on why other golfers weren't having as much fun as he was:

"They don't win as much money."

...

Chicago Bears owner George Halas, noted for his conservative approach to salaries, had this excuse when Walter Payton wanted a million-dollar contract:

"There's no way we're going to be able to pay him that. I wouldn't do it because of the morale of the team. Besides, we can't afford it."

...

Shot-putter Brian Oldfield, on why he chose to join the professional track circuit and give up his amateur status:

"When I went under the table for money, I found it already had been divided up."

...

Former All-Pro Detroit Lions defensive tackle Alex Karras, explaining what he considered the most lucrative form of writing:

"Ransom notes."

...

Beano Cook, sports publicity director for the University of Pittsburgh, on why a highly recruited basketball player ended up quitting college:

"He got tired of his dad writing him for money."

...

Bobby Riggs, 56, on why he continued his hustling ways even after losing to Billie Jean King in the "Battle of the Sexes" tennis match:

"I love money."

TAPPED OUT

Not every owner, team, coach, or athlete is always loaded with dough. Even they may run a little short— or at least make that claim. Let yourself get a little low on cash and you'll find the need to develop some excuses, too.

... ...

Charlie Theokas, New Jersey Nets general manager, on why the paychecks of three players bounced:

"Obviously, we didn't have enough money in the bank."

...

Oakland A's owner Charlie Finley, explaining why his press conference to announce reduced ticket prices was held next to the hotel pool:

"Things are so bad I couldn't afford to hold it inside the hotel."

...

Dallas Tornado soccer player Carl Bennett of the struggling North American Soccer League, on whether he could be the guest speaker at a function for $25:

"I'd really like to, but I don't think I can spare the money."

...

Mississippi State basketball coach Bob Boyd, explaining his return to coaching following a two-year retirement:

"I didn't miss the smell of the gym, the bounce of the ball, or the kids. I just ran out of money."

...

Million-dollar running back Herschel Walker, on why he declined a $500 bet with fellow pro Earl Campbell on the 1984 Cotton Bowl between their former schools, Georgia and Texas:

"I don't have any money."

BUY AND SELL

No, it's not the latest Wall Street craze for corporate mergers or takeovers. But it is enlightening to hear how those in the sports world explain the reasons behind their financial decisions. Come to think of it, they might just make more sense than those offered by Wall Street.

... ...

Dr. Martel Dailey, Gaylord Perry's family physician, on why he failed in his attempt to hold a Cy Young Award celebration for Perry in the pitcher's hometown of Williamston, North Carolina:

> *"I tried to get the Chamber of Commerce involved. But one of them said, 'Hell, he buys his tractors in Greenville.'"*

...

Elix Price, New Orleans Saints defensive tackle, on his decision to buy a disco in Yazoo City, Mississippi:

> *"I figured if I was going out on the town, I might as well spend money in my own place."*

...

George Piszek, president of Mrs. Paul's Kitchens, on why he sold the American Hockey League's Syracuse Firebirds:

> *"I guess you could say we've got other fish to fry."*

...

Jay Saldi, Dallas Cowboys tight end, on the reason for his part-ownership of a video arcade:

"I was spending too many quarters in there."

...

Kansas City Royals manager Billy Gardner, explaining his motivation for selling his bar, called the Bat Rack:

"I decided to get out when my bartender was driving a Caddy and I was driving a Chevy."

...

Lee Trevino, on his excuse for not playing the Lee Trevino model golf ball on the PGA Tour:

"I sell them."

15

The Procurement System

RECRUITING HIGH HOPES

The world's greatest coach would have trouble winning without "the horses." Thus, the ability to recruit top athletes is absolutely necessary to achieving success in college athletics. Here are some interesting explanations by coaches and athletes involved in the recruiting process.

... ...

Purdue football coach Alex Agase, on the reason he doesn't waste time recruiting in California:

"Any kid who would leave that wonderful weather is too dumb to play for us."

...

Oklahoma football coach Barry Switzer, asked in the mid-1970s to explain the effect of any NCAA probation on the school's recruiting:

"None. Because a lot of schools we recruit against are on permanent probation. They're never going to a bowl, anyway."

Tommy Vardeman, Louisiana Tech assistant basketball coach, on how the school would try to replace senior Lanky Wells, who was averaging 16 points and 4.1 fouls per game:

"Well, first, we'll have to recruit somebody with four fouls."

...

Running back Russel Charles, a Texas native, explaining his early 1970s decision to attend UCLA over the University of Texas:

"At the time I was being recruited, Texas had only one black player. I wasn't interested in being a pioneer there, so I decided to become a settler at UCLA."

...

Arkansas coach Lou Holtz, on why he almost failed to recruit one of his defensive linemen because he was weak-looking:

"If we won a game, I didn't know if he would be strong enough to carry me off the field."

...

O. J. Simpson, explaining how a horse he saw on a television broadcast of the 1963 Rose Bowl between USC and Wisconsin was the catalyst for his decision to go to USC:

"Early in the game, USC scored a touchdown and all at once, a beautiful white horse was galloping around the field. Right then and there I thought, 'That's the school I want to go to.'"

...

Quarterback John Hadl, on his decision to attend college at Kansas rather than Oklahoma:

> *"[Kansas coach] Jack Mitchell heard I was thinking about going to Oklahoma. He came over to my house at 9 o'clock at night and was still talking at two the next morning. I decided I'd better go to Kansas so I could get some sleep."*

...

Kevin Bannon, Trenton State basketball coach, explaining the benefits he got from recruiting NCAA Division III career-scoring leader Greg Grant, who had a summer job at a seafood store:

> *"My cholesterol level went down 30 percent while I recruited him."*

...

Noseguard Mike Lamb, on why he chose to attend USC:

> *"For the education, the name, to play on a winning team . . . and because [USC] Coach [Marv] Goux told me to."*

...

Oklahoma coach Barry Switzer, on the reason his Sooners have an edge in the recruiting game against in-state rival Oklahoma State:

> *"OU is easier to spell than OSU."*

DRAFT CHOICES

Draft day is a little like Christmas for general managers. The only difference is that they get to select their own presents! Of course, when the season rolls around, sometimes the enthusiasm for that draft-choice present is still there, but other times the thrill is gone.

...

Kansas All-America forward Danny Manning once plowed into the announcers' table while chasing a loose ball. Why didn't color analyst Bucky Waters get out of Manning's way like game announcer Marv Albert did?:

> *"It's always a thrill to take a charge from a top draft choice."*

...

Joe Axelson, Kansas City Kings general manager, on the reason he chose Olympic decathlon gold-medalist Bruce Jenner in the seventh round of the 1977 NBA draft:

> *"Everybody kept telling me we should draft the best available. So we did."*

...

Milt Schmidt, Washington Capitals general manager, excusing the team's season record of 9–67–5:

> *"I went for size in the draft. I figured the big thing was not to get pushed around. The trouble was the big guys I drafted—they don't like to fight."*

Cleveland Cavaliers coach Bill Fitch, gives this alibi for drafting a 5'6", 47-year-old guard, *Christian Science Monitor* sports editor Phil Elderkin:

"He was the only guy I could find who didn't have an agent, will play for the 1960 minimum, and will bring his own shoes."

...

HERE TODAY, GONE TOMORROW

How would you like to be traded? "Joe, you've been traded from our law firm here in Los Angeles to a law firm in Atlanta for a lawyer to be named later." Yikes! Yet the sports swap is still an accepted part of the game, although some veterans now receive the right of refusal. Traded players may experience feelings such as betrayal, disappointment, happiness, anger, relief, and "it's a business." The trade-makers try to fill a team need and find the right "chemistry" that might result in a championship. Here are some excuses, alibis, and explanations involving trades.

...

Milwaukee first baseman George Scott, on why he wasn't surprised when the Boston Red Sox traded him to the Brewers:

"How could I be surprised? That's the team that once traded Babe Ruth."

...

American Basketball Association veteran George Govan, on the reason he was happy to be traded to the Virginia Squires from the Utah Stars:

"None of the guys on the Utah Stars liked to play cards."

...

Pitcher Joaquin Andujar—whose tantrum got him ejected from the seventh game of the 1985 World Series—explaining why he was sent from the brewery-owned St. Louis Cardinals to the Oakland Athletics after the season:

"It was the owners, the brewery. Budweiser traded me. They're more worried about a beer can than Joaquin Andujar."

...

Seattle SuperSonics center Dennis Awtrey, on why he was traded six times in eight years:

"People like me."

...

Bum Phillips, Houston Oilers coach, on why he hadn't made any deals for awhile:

"We're not giving away any football players who could hurt us later. I don't mind people thinking I'm stupid, but I don't want to give any proof."

...

Ron Davis, Minnesota relief pitcher, explaining why he didn't understand how his comments about the Twins' front office were played up in the newspapers:

"All I said was that the trades were stupid and dumb and they took that and blew it all out of proportion."

...

Atlanta Hawks general manager Stan Kasten, on the reason he was having difficulty making trades with other NBA teams:

"They all want to give me bad players, and I've got enough of those."

...

Milwaukee general manager Frank "Trader" Lane, explaining why the lowly Brewers didn't execute a single trade during the winter baseball meetings:

"We didn't want to weaken the rest of the league."

...

Burt Hawkins, Texas Rangers traveling secretary, on why he thought the ball club would show improvement:

"We've traded away so many of our old players we've weakened the rest of the league."

...

Longtime Golden State Warriors center Nate Thurmond, explaining his feelings about being swapped to the Chicago Bulls:

"I've read over the years that I was as much a Bay Area landmark as the Golden Gate Bridge. But I'm going, and that bridge isn't going anywhere."

...

Charlie Finley, on why he traded Oakland A's manager Chuck Tanner to the Pittsburgh Pirates for catcher Manny Sanguillen and $100,000:

"If I'm going to run a finishing school for managers, I want to be paid for it."

...

New York Rangers general manger and coach Phil Esposito, on his motivation for making so many trades in his first year at the team's helm:

"I want to win now. I might be hit by a bus tomorrow."

...

Sacramento Kings coach Jerry Reynolds, explaining the results of management's decision to trade centers Joe Kleine and LaSalle Thompson without receiving a center in return:

"If we had one more center, we'd have one."

...

Tug McGraw, Philadelphia relief pitcher, explaining to his new teammates why the New York Mets had sent him to the Phillies:

"I was the only complete ass they had. Here, I just fit right in."

...

Buffalo Braves rookie Adrian Dantley—who grew up in the Washington, D.C., area—on why he would enjoy being traded to the Washington Bullets:

"If I was with the Bullets, my mom could do my cooking."

MANAGEMENT DECISIONS

Do the "Big Cheeses" of the world always know what's going on? Does your boss? Often they do; sometimes they don't. While bosses are paid to make decisions, occasionally they operate as if they were out in left field. Here are several explanations involving bosses and key management decisions and policy.

...

New York Giants president Wellington Mara, explaining what's next after firing head coach John McVay and accepting the resignation of director of operations Andy Robustelli:

"Our first move will be to decide what our first move will be."

...

Bill Lucas, Atlanta Braves general manager, explaining what he would do after some players refused to admit women sportswriters into the locker room for postgame interviews:

"I think we've got a policy on this. Now, I've got to find out what it is."

...

Veteran infielder Bobby Valentine, trying to fathom the New York Mets' explanation for releasing him during spring training:

"When I was released [manager] Joe Torre told me he didn't like the way I moved at second base. I haven't been at second base all spring."

...

Nebraska coach Bob Devaney, on why he and three assistant coaches showed up at the Extra Point Club luncheon in Lincoln after the No. 1 Cornhuskers' upset loss to the UCLA Bruins:

"We drew straws to see who would come down. The four of us lost."

...

Detroit Pistons coach Scotty Robertson, on the reason he had no preference whether team general manager Jack McCloskey called heads or tails in a flip for the NBA's No. 1 draft pick:

"That's his job."

16
The Skills and Scouting Report

PRACTICE MAKES PERFECT

Practice, practice, practice! That's the lesson for those who wish to excel on the athletic field. Ask Magic Johnson, Larry Bird, Joe Montana, or any star. While diligent practice may put some athletes on the road to success, other athletes may wind up using practice sessions as an excuse.

... ...

Dr. Delano Meriwether—a 28-year-old sprinter whose practice time was limited to just two hours each week—on how he managed to capture sprint titles in both the U.S. indoor and outdoor national track and field championships:

"For national meets I practice three hours."

...

New Orleans coach Bum Phillips, recounting Saints running back Chuck Muncie's excuses for missing practice:

"He went to five grandmothers' funerals."

Former heavyweight champion Floyd Patterson, after being sent to the canvas by light heavyweight Harold Carter during a sparring session:

"I go down all the time in workouts."

...

When University of Minnesota kicker Mike Reid received a 15-yard penalty for catching his own windblown kickoff, Golden Gophers coach Murray Warmath explained:

"We never practice that play, because we never thought it could happen."

...

Former NFL star Alex Karras on his golf game:

"My best score ever is 103. But I've only been playing 15 years."

...

USC coach John McKay, on why he didn't have his College All-Stars prepare with two-a-day drills for their exhibition game against the Super Bowl winner:

"One practice a day is all I can stand."

PASSING AND CATCHING

Passing and catching are among the basic skills of sports such as basketball and football. Of course, the successful execution of these skills is often more difficult. That ineptitude must be excused or explained. Here are some choice excuses for occasions when the passing and catching game left something to be desired.

... ...

Philadelphia 76ers rookie Bud Ogden, explaining to a sportswriter why he had thrown him the ball on press row during a fast break:

"You were open."

...

Boston Celtic center Greg Kite, on why he passed the ball to referee Paul Mihalak after 7'7" Manute Bol of the Washington Bullets shut off his attempted drive to the basket:

"I heard Mihalak can stick the jumper."

...

When Cleveland defensive back Frank Minnifield failed to find running room on an interception return, he lateraled the ball to Browns defensive back Hanford Dixon. What was Minnifield's excuse to coach Marty Schottenheimer?:

"I'm running and Hanford won't block anybody. So I figure, I'm gonna give Hanford the ball and let them tackle Hanford."

...

David McWilliams, Texas Tech football coach, explaining how many of his team's 72 passes in its spring game were completed:

"We worked on throwing in the spring. We'll work on catching in the fall."

...

New England Patriots coach Ron Erhardt, on why his receivers were dropping so many passes despite being coached by sure-handed Hall of Fame receiver Raymond Berry:

> *"Raymond is coaching them, not catching them."*

STRENGTHS AND WEAKNESSES

Players and coaches occasionally have an interesting way of evaluating their pluses and minuses. They may not always express this evaluation in quite the correct manner, but they try. Here are some explanations that are intriguing.

... ...

Mark Snow, New Mexico basketball player, describing his athletic skills:

> *"Strength is my biggest weakness."*

...

Arkansas football coach Frank Broyles, on the Razorbacks' outlook for the season:

> *"Our strength is that we don't have any weaknesses. Our weakness is that we don't have any real strengths."*

...

David Thompson of the Denver Nuggets, on his basketball skills:

> *"Ball handling and dribbling are my strongest weaknesses."*

Buck Williams, New Jersey Nets forward, explaining why he averaged barely one assist a game during the 1982 season:

"I knew those guys were out there. I just didn't know where."

...

Darnell Hillman of the NBA Kansas City Kings, explaining his strengths and weaknesses:

"The places where I need work are on my inside and outside games."

...

Amateur golfer Bob Clampett, on the strongest element of his game:

"Luck."

DON'T PASS ME BY

Remember that ball hog on your grade school team who never learned what a P-A-S-S was on the basketball court? Once you had graciously passed the ball—in the true team spirit—you darn well knew the ball wasn't coming back into your hands again. The professional and college ranks have players who could care less about assists, although every once in awhile a previously lost soul is saved from permanent gunnerhood.

... ...

Manute Bol, 7'7" Washington Bullets center, after it took him 692 minutes of playing time to get his first assist of the season:

"What do you expect? I'm not Magic Johnson."

...

UCLA Bruins basketball guard Pooh Richardson, on the reason for his transformation from a gunner in junior high school to a playmaker in high school:

"My cousin was on the team. I had to pass him the ball or he'd get mad."

Kansas City Kings point guard Nate Archibald, on why he was taking more shots than he did in the previous season:

"We don't have that many good shooters. There aren't many guys to pass to, so I pass to me."

17
Physical Measures

THE HEAVYWEIGHT DIVISION

Sports has its weighty matters and heavy side. Believe it or not, all athletes are not necessarily interested in losing fat and putting on muscle. Nor are they all interested in taking on heavy assignments. In other words, losing weight is one thing; lifting it is another. Here are some excuses regarding their behavior in heavy and weighty situations.

... ...

Former SMU hurdler Bob Johnson, on why he never began a weight-lifting program:

"I tried to, but I couldn't get them out of my car."

...

Utah Jazz coach Frank Layden, explaining his attempts to slim down his 300-pound physique at a weight-loss clinic:

"It's hard to be fit as a fiddle when you're shaped like a cello."

...

Rookie Houston infielder Ernie Fazio, on why he switched from a 33-ounce bat to a lighter, 29-ounce model:

"It's easier to carry back to the dugout after I strike out."

...

Washington Redskins quarterback Sonny Jurgensen, carrying an ample midsection, explaining what he does to stay in shape during the off-season:

"Obviously, nothing."

...

Center Mel Turpin, on his excuse for joining Utah weighing 280 pounds—20 pounds more than the Cleveland Cavaliers reported he weighed before trading him to the Jazz:

"I love airplane food."

...

Frank Howard, after managing the San Diego Padres the previous season, on how he cut his weight to 275 pounds as a New York Mets coach:

"You don't eat as well on a coach's salary."

...

Dallas Cowboys coach Tom Landry, on the reason he no longer was wearing his Super Bowl ring the year after winning the Big One:

"It's too heavy."

...

Husky Atlanta Braves relief pitcher Terry Forster, on why he decided to go to a fat farm:

"A waist is a terrible thing to mind."

...

Heavyset Frank Layden, on why he doesn't need to lift weights:

"I get a lot of practice just lifting myself out of bed each day."

...

Olympic 100-meter breaststroke gold-medalist Steve Lundquist, explaining the necessity of his pre-Olympic Trials crash diet:

"I was so fat I needed two mirrors."

...

During a PGA Seniors golf tournament, Billy Casper had this explanation for his increasing waistline:

"Like a lot of fellows around here, I have a furniture problem. My chest has fallen into my drawers."

...

Pedro Guerrero, traded from Los Angeles to St. Louis, on the reason he changed his uniform number to 28 from the first jersey the Cardinals gave him, namely, number 43:

"It was too heavy."

...

Sonny Jurgensen, explaining why he didn't pursue a basketball career after starring on the court during high school:

"I grew out instead of up."

...

Charlie Kerfeld, former Houston Astros reliever, on how he was able to reduce his weight from 275 pounds to 245 pounds after his demotion to the minor leagues:

"Meal money in the Southern League is $13 a day."

...

Don Baird, star pole-vaulter for Long Beach State, explaining how weight training helped him:

"I've got the weights sitting on the floor of my apartment. I wake up in the morning and look at them and that makes me feel stronger."

...

Beth Heiden, world speed-skating champion, on the most difficult part of her sport:

"The hardest part . . . is the victory wreath. Boy, those wreaths are really heavy."

LONG AND SHORT OF IT

One great thing about sports is that it offers enough room for both the tall and the small. A Spud Webb can be on the same court with a Manute Bol. Of course, advantages and disadvantages exist for both. And when it comes to size and height, nothing is ever quite perfect. To size it all up, here are excuses and explanations concerning the vagaries of height.

Manute Bol, 7'7" center, on why his passport only listed him as 5'2":

"They measured me when I was sitting down."

...

Center Tom Burleson, 7'4" member of the 1972 U.S. Olympic basketball team, on the reason he wasn't bothered by comments that he was actually 7'2¾" when measured barefoot:

"I am 7'4" with my shoes on, and I always play with my shoes on."

...

Nate Thurmond, Golden State Warriors 6'11" center, on the reason he tabled ideas of a baseball career:

"I gave up when I realized I couldn't hit the high fastball."

...

Philadelphia 76ers 6'11" forward Darryl Dawkins, on how he developed his good outside shot:

"Where I come from the dudes are so big I'm only allowed to play guard in the summer."

...

Elvin Hayes, 6'10" Washington Bullets forward, when asked if he was a basketball player:

"No, I clean giraffe ears."

...

University of Houston 7' center Akeem Olajuwon, excusing himself for a poor first-half performance against small-college underdog St. Mary's of Texas:

"All those little guys kept hitting my hands. And one guy kept running underneath me."

...

Johnny Kerr, who was a 6'9" center and later coach for the Chicago Bulls, asked by a woman if he was a basketball player:

"No, ma'am, I'm a jockey for a dinosaur."

...

Eddie Dibbs, 5'7" professional tennis player, on why he declined an invitation from 6'10" NBA forward Bob McAdoo for a little game of 1–on–1:

"The closer I got, the taller he looked."

...

Alex Hannum, Philadelphia 76ers coach, on why he was listed at 6'8" as a player but only 6'7" as a coach:

"I got bald."

...

Chuck Wepner, explaining how his boxing career helped stimulate his growth:

"I was 6'1" when I started fighting, but with all those uppercuts, I'm up to 6'5"."

...

San Diego Padres hurler Randy Jones, on why he had yet to win a game in Busch Stadium, home of the St. Louis Cardinals:

"The mound's too high."

...

Joe Dial, after setting the prep pole-vault record at 17–9½, explaining why he didn't go on to break the 18-foot barrier even though he thought he could:

"They couldn't set the standards any higher."

Thirteen-year-old soccer player Matt McDonagh of Highland Catholic School in St. Paul, Minnesota, on his team's loss to Presentation in the city playoffs:

"I knew we were in trouble when we got there and their cheerleaders were bigger than us."

...

Duke women's basketball coach Debbie Leonard, trying to explain the team's 103–39 shellacking by Maryland:

"The worst thing our players did was fail to grow taller."

...

Tom Lovat, Stanford offensive line coach, on why many of the team's running backs were less than six feet tall:

"Because our line can only make holes under six feet high."

...

Longtime Seattle sportscaster Wayne Cody, 5'10" and 262 pounds, explaining his build:

"My doctor said I just wasn't tall enough. My weight is perfect for someone who is 13'9"."

...

Eddie LeBaron, explaining how he wound up as one of the shortest quarterbacks ever to play in the NFL:

"I started out at 5'10" and wound up at 5'7"."

...

Hugh Durham, Georgia basketball coach, on why young Bulldog guard Darryl Lenard's reported height decreased from 5'8" in high school to 5'6" in college:

"He shrank during shipping."

...

Hugh Durham, on his tall Florida State squad's tough time against much smaller Georgia Southern:

"It was tough to match up with them—they're too small."

...

Baltimore Colt Howard Stevens, 5'5", 165-pound kick returner, explaining his build:

"I'm not small, I'm short. If I were six feet, I'd weigh 220 pounds."

...

Five-foot-four Freddie Patek of the Kansas City Royals, on how he felt about being the major league's smallest player:

"It feels a helluva lot better than being the smallest player in the minors."

...

University of Washington basketball coach Marv Harshman, explaining his preference for size to speed:

"Quick guys get tired. Big guys don't shrink."

...

Jockey Ron Turcotte, who rode Secretariat to the Triple Crown, on why he didn't worry about his small stature:

"When I'm on a horse I'm as tall as anybody."

SPEED RATING

Sports has its share of speed measures. Football has its 40-yard dash, track has the 100-meter run, baseball features fastballs by the likes of Nolan Ryan, Roger Clemens, and Dwight Gooden, and the Indianapolis 500 has race-car drivers going more than 220 miles per hour to qualify. Here are some quotes from both the hare and the tortoise side of motion measuring sticks.

... ...

Richard Petty, explaining how fast he would need to go to capture a 500-mile race at Ontario Motor Speedway:

"That all depends on how fast the car in second plans on going."

...

Former All-America Washington State quarterback Jack Thompson, not exactly the most fleet of foot, on how he managed to run for 10 touchdowns during his college career:

"It's amazing what the human body can do when chased by a bigger human body."

...

New York Jets quarterback Joe Namath, after making a 39-yard run against the Oakland Raiders despite his bad knees:

"When Big Ben Davidson is after me, I'm a 9.2 sprinter."

...

Cincinnati Reds outfielder Ken Griffey, on the reason he runs so fast:

"If you grew up in a ghetto, you'd be fast, too."

...

Sprinter Steve Williams, on how growing up in the New York's Bronx helped him develop into one of the world's fastest humans during the early 1970s:

"Where I lived, you had to be fast to keep living."

...

Vanderbilt defensive end Glenn Watson, explaining why he changed his jersey number from 92 to 36:

"I look a lot faster when I wear 36."

...

Houston Oilers running back Earl Campbell, excusing himself for not divulging his time in the 40-yard dash—football's speed measurement standard:

"I never run it. I might embarrass myself."

...

Louie Kelcher, San Diego Chargers defensive tackle, explaining his lack of swiftness in the 40:

"If I have to run 40 yards to catch somebody, I ain't gonna catch him nohow."

...

Renowned fastball pitcher Ron Guidry of the New York Yankees, on his failure to develop a good change-up:

"I can't get the thing under 86 mph."

...

Chicago White Sox pitcher Dave LaPoint, on why not being blessed with a Sandy Koufax–type fastball worked to his advantage:

"Teams can't prepare for me in batting practice. They can't find anyone who throws as slow as I do."

...

Race-car driver Arlene Hiss, on the reason she crashed during practice for a stock-car event at Ontario Motor Speedway:

"I was just trying to get through a 136 mile-per-hour turn going 140."

...

Stock-car driver Donnie Allison, on why he couldn't go any faster than 138 miles per hour during qualifying for the American 500:

"My heart wouldn't stand it."

...

SMU quarterback Chuck Hixson, who was leading the NCAA in total offense and passing, explaining how a slow runner like himself had rushed for five touchdowns:

"The defense doesn't know whether I'm sprinting out or walking over to talk to Coach [Hayden] Fry."

...

Football broadcaster Hank Stram, offering his explanation on the speed of San Francisco 49ers quarterback Steve Spurrier:

"He has very deceptive speed. He's a lot slower than he looks."

...

California Angels first baseman Ron Fairly, 40, on the reason he hadn't lost any of his speed:

"There was nothing to lose."

...

Jon Sinclair, winner of Atlanta's Peachtree Road Race, on why he eased up four miles into the race when he found out he was running alone:

"I didn't want to run by myself, so I slowed down."

...

Hall of Fame pitcher Lefty Gomez, on the secret of his success:

"Clean living and a fast outfield."

18
The Body Human

BODY PARTS

Eyes, ears, nose, legs, face, arms. You would be surprised how industrious sports figures are at utilizing
just about every part of the body for their alibis and
explanations. Perhaps their imaginative answers will
help give you a little needed body English the next time
you can use an excuse.

... ...

Former major-league umpire Ron Luciano, on why he
failed as an NBC-TV baseball color analyst:

"I've got a face made for radio."

...

Gordie Howe, Hall of Fame hockey player, asked if he
had ever broken his nose:

"No, but 11 other guys did."

...

Oakland manager Billy Martin, on why he was having more success teaching baseball fundamentals to the Athletics than he did teaching to the Yankees:

"I taught in New York, but not too many listened. The players here have bigger ears."

...

Winnipeg Jets defenseman Randy Carlyle, on why he is one of the few NHL players who doesn't wear a helmet:

"The guys tell me I have nothing to protect. No brain, no pain."

...

Danny Ozark, Philadelphia Phillies manager, on why he thought Jerry Dale was a great umpire:

"He's got 20–20 ears."

...

California Angels TV announcer Bob Starr, with this alibi for misidentifying a relief pitcher warming up in the bullpen:

"I was looking through my eyes rather than the TV monitor."

...

Tennis star Martina Navratilova, on why she decided against taking out a Lloyd's of London insurance policy on her left arm:

"They wanted an arm and a leg for it."

...

Kent Tekulve, Pittsburgh Pirates relief pitcher, on never having arm trouble:

"Maybe it's because I have no muscles in my arm."

...

Golfer Johnny Miller, explaining his prolonged slump on the pro tour:

"My suppleness was the biggest thing I lost. When you get around 30 years old your muscles start to get tighter, it seems."

...

Utility outfielder and pinch-hitter John Lowenstein of the Baltimore Orioles, on how he stays ready until called upon late in the game:

"I flush the john between innings to keep my wrists strong."

...

Gordie Howe of the Houston Aeros, on why his 900th career goal was celebrated with mere handshakes:

"When I scored my 800th, I tried to leap up in the air. I came right down on my butt."

...

University of Kansas basketball coach Larry Brown, on how the team's Allen Fieldhouse seats only 15,200 fans compared to announced crowds of more than 17,000 during Wilt Chamberlain days:

"Bigger fannies."

...

Minnesota quarterback Fran Tarkenton excusing himself after fans booed him for failing to lead the Vikings to a touchdown:

"I've been playing this game for 18 years and I haven't yet figured a way to get into the end zone when you're on your rear end."

...

Chicago White Sox star Dick Allen, explaining his philosophy of taking as little batting practice as possible:

"Your body is just like a bar of soap. It gradually wears down from repeated use."

...

Kansas City catcher John Wathan, on why Royals relief ace Dan Quisenberry never wears down:

"There's nobody there to get tired. It'd be like asking a broom if it was getting tired."

...

UCLA forward Kiki Vandeweghe, asked by an Eastern sportswriter why he didn't have a tan like everyone else from Southern California's Pacific Palisades:

"I guess there's not a lot of sun in gyms."

...

Jim Goldrick, University of Texas weight event star, on why discus throwers often wear sweat pants while throwing:

"In my case, it's because my legs are thin, weak and pale. Girls do not whistle or breathe heavily when I remove my sweat bottoms."

...

Gordie Howe, explaining why he didn't know if Philadelphia Flyer Reggie Fleming was a "hard-nosed" player:

"I never felt his nose."

...

Winston Bennett, University of Kentucky star basketball forward, explaining why he was ready for action after a knee operation:

"I've never had major knee surgery on any other part of my body."

...

Tom Penders, University of Texas basketball coach, on why he didn't make any predictions about the team after his hiring:

"A good friend of mine in coaching told me a long time ago the best way to save face is to keep the lower half of it shut."

DISHPAN HANDS

I bet you didn't realize the impact that washing dishes has made on sports. Excuses and explanations involving dishes are more than the sole realm of kids serving as human dishwashers in households without electric ones.

... ...

When Alvin Dark joined the San Francisco Giants as their manager, his wife was asked about the former major leaguer's excuse for not helping her with the dishes:

*"He always said he couldn't let his hands get too
soft to hold the bat."*

Tight end Kellen Winslow, pass catching wizard for
the San Diego Chargers, on how he developed his soft
hands:

*"I was the oldest of three brothers and one of
my jobs was to wash the dishes."*

…

When John Lloyd was married to Chris Evert, he was
asked during a tournament why three fingers of his
right hand were taped:

*"My hands are very soft because of all the dishes
I have to wash."*

…

Ivory Crockett, the first man to run nine seconds flat in
the 100-yard dash, on why he thought his mother
named him Ivory:

*"She was doing a lot of dishes while she was
pregnant."*

…

LPGA rookie Patty Sheehan, on the reason she became
a professional golfer:

*"It wasn't much fun being an amateur. I got
tired of polishing the silverware."*

HAIR-RAISING TALES

From mustaches and beards to long hair or shaved heads, men face a plethora of hair-raising, or -losing, choices. To grow the long locks and look like a rock 'n' roll star or to take the Kareem Abdul-Jabbar route? To Fu Manchu or to leave that caterpillar off your upper lip? To "toupee" or go for the natural look? Here are a multitude of excuses and reasons behind the hairy tales of some sports figures.

... ...

Dallas Cowboys quarterback Roger Staubach, on why his mustache only lasted a short time:

"Kids were coming up and asking me if I was a kicker."

...

Swimming star Mark Spitz, on why he grew a mustache for the 1972 Summer Olympic Games:

"It helps keep the water out of my nose."

...

Pro golfer Bunky Henry, on the reason he finally cut his long hair:

"I was taking a shower and found a pencil behind my ear. I have no idea how long it was there."

...

After making 36 errors at third base the previous season, Atlanta Braves infielder Darrell Evans explained why he had grown a beard and long hair for a try at first base:

"If I botch it up at first, at least nobody will know who I am."

...

Detroit Tigers pitcher Mark "The Bird" Fidrych, explaining why he got a haircut:

"I couldn't see over to first base."

...

Montreal Expos pitcher Bill "Spaceman" Lee, on why he stopped shaving:

"I decided to stop shaving in order to save my arm. You know, all that lifting up and down. It's wear and tear."

...

Bill Lee, on why he later decided to shave off the beard he had been growing for more than a year:

"I want to remain anonymous for the next couple of months."

...

A young Jack Nicklaus, on why he didn't bother to get a haircut for three months:

"Biggest waste of time in the world is getting a haircut or stopping for gas."

...

Miami Dolphins placekicker Garo Yepremian, on the reason he shaved off his bushy mustache:

"My boys were getting rashes when I kissed them."

...

Al Hrabosky, St. Louis Cardinals relief pitcher, on why he grew a Fu Manchu mustache:

"I try to intimidate the batter. I'm not going out there looking like a neat little country boy."

...

Darryl Dawkins of the Philadelphia 76ers, explaining his shaved head:

"I got in a bad accident and broke all my hairs."

...

Jack McKeon, Kansas City Royals manager, on his new mustache:

"I grew it when we were dealing for Catfish Hunter."

...

Shot-putter Al Feuerbach, who once professed that long hair gave him more strength, on why he opted to cut his hair short:

"It's part of my new discipline. It's some psychological thing. Anyway, I was getting hair in my hands when I was throwing."

...

Third baseman Bob Horner of the Atlanta Braves, on the disappearance of his beard:

"I've been traveling so much I haven't had time to grow it."

...

Heavyweight boxer Earnie Shavers, on why he shaved his head:

"You know, we all look alike."

...

Green Bay Packer wide receiver Steve Odom, on the reason he came to training camp with a shaved head:

"Basically, I just wanted to give my head a chance to breathe."

...

Boston Red Sox pitcher Luis Tiant, on why he started losing his hair when he pitched in Mexico:

"My hair got thin from too many home runs, I think."

...

Balding Atlanta Braves manager Joe Torre, on the reason he calls his hair style a "Watergate":

"I cover up everything I can."

...

Richard Byrd, rookie Houston Oilers linebacker, after getting his head shaved along with a group of teammates:

"I guess it was voluntary. There were 10 guys around me. So I volunteered."

Oakland A's relief pitcher Steve Ontiveros, on why his shaky season start resulted in the elimination of his mustache:

"It wasn't producing, so I sent it out."

...

ABC sportscaster Keith Jackson, explaining his new beard:

"I promised my wife I would keep it a year and hide my double chin."

...

Greg Pruitt, Cleveland Browns running back, on the reason attempts to heal an ankle injury resulted in a trim for his Afro:

"It's an old remedy my grandmother told me about. If you're hurting, get a haircut and the ailment will improve."

...

Texas Longhorns coach Abe Lemons, after an upset loss to the University of Pacific, on why Tigers 6'9" center Ron Cornelius got loose for 34 points:

"Our guys just never figured out he was the tall guy with the mustache."

PARALYZING MOMENTS

Aggressive players may sometimes make mistakes, but coaches usually applaud their ability to take action and risks. In other words, act decisively. Sometimes people freeze and don't act at all. Here are some excuses and explanations involving those moments of paralysis.

Seattle SuperSonics coach Bill Russell, explaining why he sat quietly while the New Jersey Nets raced to a 17-point lead in the game's first seven minutes:

"When you're in a complete state of panic, you can't move."

...

New York Tech freshman defensive back John Smith, burned on a 63-yard pass play by Rensselaer Tech, explaining to coach Marty Senall why he froze:

"My contact lens had popped out and I covered it with my foot, waiting for a time to put it back. If I had left that spot, I never would have found it again in that grass. My parents would have killed me for losing it."

...

Pittsburgh general manager Joe Brown, on the only times the Pirates' free-swinging catcher Manny Sanguillen takes a pitch:

"When Manny takes a pitch, it's either a wild pitch or paralysis just set in."

...

Tommy Prothro, Los Angeles Rams coach, explaining the peril of viewing too many game films:

"There is a danger of paralysis through analysis."

JEEPERS, CREEPERS, WHERE'D YOU GET THOSE PEEPERS?

"Open your eyes, ump!" Yes, sight is indeed an important part of sports, whether it's calling balls and strikes, hitting a major league fastball, making a "blind" pass for a dunk, or trying to pick up the blitz. Here are some quotes that utilize sight or the lack of it as excuses and explanations.

... ...

Pacific Coast League umpire Ralph DeLeonardis, on charges he blew an easy play at home plate:

"Well, I blew it the way I saw it."

...

Baltimore exotic dancer Blaze Starr, on her excuse for spurning a request to "streak" on a horse at Pimlico:

"It was a long shot and it wasn't wearing blinkers."

...

AL umpire Ron Luciano, explaining why hunting isn't his sport:

"I like to hunt, but I never hit anything. I don't see too well."

...

Philadelphia Phillies pitcher Don Carman, on whether his minuscule .024 batting average might be attributed to trouble with his eyesight:

"I'm seeing the ball real good. I just can't hit it."

...

Philadelphia Phillies pitcher Steve Carlton, on whether his entire life flashed in front of his eyes when a line drive nailed him on the neck:

"All I saw was [NL President] Chub Feeney's name and 'Sewn in Haiti.'"

...

New England Patriots quarterback Jim Plunkett, on who stuck him with the hardest hit during his rookie season:

"I don't know. I keep my eyes closed when I'm hit."

...

Harley Duncan, licensing bureau official for the State of Kansas, on why he allowed George Brett to skip the eye test while renewing his driver's license:

"If he can hit .350, we figured he could see."

...

Jack Nicklaus, discussing the status of his golf game:

"I got contact lenses so I could see. Now I can see and I can't make anything."

...

After being ejected by umpire Ken Burkhart for arguing a ball-four call, veteran major league pitcher Ryne Duren offered the umpire his glasses. When Duren yelled and screamed, Burkhart asked for an explanation:

"I asked why he was yelling so loud, and he said, 'I just wanted to see if your hearing was as bad as your sight.' "

...

Pro golfer Gary Player, explaining why he barely missed making a 197-yard hole-in-one at a PGA tournament:

"I couldn't read the break in the green from the tee."

Ron Luciano, on one reason his retirement from the umpiring profession made him happy:

"For one thing, now I can wear my glasses when I'm in a restaurant having trouble reading the menu."

...

New York pitcher Tommy John, on why he didn't accompany some of his Yankee teammates to the musical "Damn Yankees" in Toronto:

"Why should I? I've been seeing the damn Yankees all season."

...

Following a player complaint that he was much too distant to see a play he had called, umpire Bruce Froemming retorted:

"The sun is 93 million miles away and I can see it."

ALL WHITE NOW

"White man's disease" has always been a convenient excuse for those embarrassed by their lack of jumping ability on the basketball court. I guess great black athletes like Michael Jordan, Magic Johnson, and Bo Jackson could make anyone seem inferior physically. Here are some other choice alibis used by Caucasians in the sports world.

... ...

Cotton Fitzsimmons, Kansas City Kings coach, on why he wasn't interested in selecting Larry Bird in the 1978 NBA draft:

"I already have two white guys on my team."

...

Dave Collins, Cincinnati Reds white speedster, on how he managed to win the South Dakota state 100-yard dash during his high school days:

"There's lots of white guys up there."

...

Former major leaguer Richie Asburn, centerfielder for the 1950 NL champion Philadelphia Phillies, on why that group never captured another pennant:

"We were all white."

19
Put On the Sick and Tired List

IN SICKNESS AND IN HEALTH

"I'm sick" is probably the most popular excuse used to skip school or work. Naturally, sports figures sometimes utilize this theme. However, they bring their own innovative, inventive twists to this long-practiced art, raising the illness excuse to new levels.

... ...

Bill "Spaceman" Lee, Boston Red Sox pitcher, explaining the ailment that prematurely ended his vacation to China:

> *"They have a lot of germs over there, and since everyone over there is so small, I got them first."*

...

Player-coach Dave Cowens of the Boston Celtics, on his decision to participate only as a player during the next season:

> *"I decided not to coach because after games you have a sore throat and a headache."*

Minnesota Twins scout Ellis Clary, explaining why he didn't want a pacemaker after suffering a heart attack:

"The doctor wanted me to have a pacemaker put in, but I refused because my brother had one installed and every time he sneezes the garage door flies open."

...

Willis Reed, assistant coach for the lowly Sacramento Kings, telling a player the reason he was feeling ill:

"I've been watching you guys and you made me sick."

...

Fiery San Diego Padres manager Larry Bowa, in a bad mood after his team's slow start, on why he pitched batting practice wearing a heavy warmup jacket despite 80-degree weather:

"I was trying to have a stroke, but it didn't work."

...

John Ralston, ex-Denver Broncos head coach, on why he was ousted:

"I left because of illness and fatigue. The fans were sick and tired of me."

...

Kansas basketball coach Larry Brown, explaining how flu-stricken forward Calvin Thompson managed to go on a scoring spree:

"I think when he hit three shots in a row, that cleared his nostrils a bit."

...

Detroit Tigers catcher Marty Castillo, on his remedy for curing his 1-for-24 batting slump:

"My bats are in Mexico undergoing Laetrile treatments."

...

Pittsburgh Steelers quarterback Terry Bradshaw, on not having his tonsils removed when he had tonsilitis:

"God gave them to me. If He didn't want me to have them, He wouldn't have given them to me."

...

Ernie Camacho, Cleveland Indians relief pitcher, on the cause of the headaches he sometimes gets during pitching stints:

"I never blink when I'm on the mound, and that creates pressure on my temples. I blink all the time off the mound, and I don't have headaches then."

...

Billy Casper shot a 5-over-par 75 in a tournament and explained that he had an upset stomach from some sausage he ate in a motel coffee shop. But fellow golfer Miller Barber offered his own explanation:

"Bad sausage and five bogeys will give you a stomachache every time."

...

San Fernando Valley College distance runner Jon Sutherland, on the reason he avoided running the 880-yard dash in competition:

"Why train for 20 hours a week and get a tremendous headache in less than two minutes?"

When 7-year-old Philadelphia elementary school student Brian Pollack wanted to keep an appointment at the Spectrum to see Julius "Dr. J" Erving and the 76ers play the Atlanta Hawks, he brought his teacher the following note:

"Please excuse Brian at 1:00 P.M. . . . He has to see the doctor."

...

Cleveland relief pitcher Jamie Easterly, after receiving treatment for a rash, explaining his new fitness regimen to Indians manager Pat Corrales:

"The doctor told me I can't run for the rest of the season. And I can drink only Chivas Regal."

THE INJURY REPORT

Injuries are part of every sport and are to be avoided at all costs. Players hate to be injured, but will often attempt to play despite their physical condition. That's because it sometimes hurts worse to sit on the sidelines. Coaches hate injuries, too, but will be coy about which of their charges are slowed. Team physicians and doctors, while usually doing an admirable job, may inadvertently contribute to an occasional injury problem if they're not careful.

... ...

New York Jets coach Weeb Ewbank, on why star quarterback Joe Namath missed a practice:

"I wouldn't say that Joe has a sore arm, per se, but his arm is kind of sore."

...

Tampa Bay punter Dave Green, shaken up and prone on the field following a punt, explaining the trouble to a team physician who came out and knelt down:

"You're kneeling on my knee."

...

San Diego Chargers halfback Keith Lincoln, on the reason he played in the American Football League All-Star Game despite an injured knee:

"A low IQ helps."

...

Herschel Walker's mother, Christine, explaining that possible injury to her son wasn't the reason she didn't want him playing football as an eighth grader, but that it was:

"So he wouldn't hurt anybody else."

...

Miami Dolphins coach Don Shula, on which leg All-Pro receiver Paul Warfield hurt during practice for Super Bowl VIII against the Minnesota Vikings:

"I dunno. It's one of the two."

...

Detroit Tigers manager Sparky Anderson, explaining his unique theory about pain while discussing a player's shoulder injury:

"There's nothing wrong with his shoulder except some pain—and pain don't hurt you."

...

Donnie Martin, Long Beach State freshman basketball guard, asked by center Dwight Jones how his injured shoulder felt:

"It only hurts when I'm on the bench."

MR. FATIGUE

"I'm too tired" can serve as a good excuse to get out of work around the house. It works well in the sports world, too. Despite being well-conditioned physical specimens, top athletes can become plain tuckered out and pooped, both physically and mentally. Thus, fatigue is readily applied to excuse and explain a variety of actions by athletes and even by coaches.

... ...

New York Yankees manager Billy Martin, explaining why he looked tired:

"If you'd been hanging around Mickey Mantle, you'd be tired, too."

...

New York Giants coach Bill Parcells, on how he knew his team was tired during training camp:

"When Lawrence Taylor is in bed at 10:30, you know they're tired."

...

Olympic hurdler Greg Foster, on why his football career as a wide receiver in high school only lasted about two weeks:

"I got tired of running down the field and having the ball land 30 yards behind me."

...

Muhammad Ali, on spending so much time against the ropes in a 15-round loss to Joe Frazier:

"That's where tired men go."

...

Whitey Herzog, and his alibi for only hitting .258 playing center field for the Washington Senators between slow outfield teammates Roy Sievers and Jim Lemon:

"By the time I got to bat, I was too tired to hit."

...

Kansas football coach Don Fambrough, on his motivation for deciding to give his Jayhawks three days off:

"I needed the rest."

...

LPGA professional Robyn Dummett, explaining the difficulties of playing the rolling hills course at the Wheeling, West Virginia, Ladies Classic:

"When you get to your ball you're too tired to hit it."

...

Football great Bronco Nagurski, on why players of his era didn't have end-zone touchdown celebrations like the players of today:

"We were too tired. We used to play on offense and defense."

...

Former New York Yankee pitching great Whitey Ford, who utilized mud and scuff balls during his career, on why he took up scuffing again:

"I'm tired of losing Old-Timers' Games."

...

Buffalo Braves forward Bob McAdoo, on his excuse for entering the NBA's hardship draft after junior year at North Carolina:

> *"I just got tired of walking. That's a very large campus."*

...

Oklahoma linebacker Dante Jones, on his lack of any celebration after going 58 yards for a touchdown with a fumble recovery:

> *"I had planned to do a little celebrating in the end zone, but by the time I got there, I was too tired to dance."*

...

When the Oakland A's became outfielder Willie Crawford's fourth team of the season, he explained why he chose 99 as his uniform number:

> *"I got tired of asking for a number that was already worn by someone else. I knew there'd be no problem with 99."*

...

Dana Kunze, whose high dive of 158 feet set a world record, on the toughest part of the dive:

> *"Climbing the ladder. That's 160 feet or so, and that's tiring."*

...

Louis Breeden, Cincinnati Bengals defensive back, on the reason he neglected to spike the ball after he scored on a 102-yard interception return:

> *"I was too tired."*

...

When Texas pitcher Jim Kern and manager Pat Corrales met on the mound, Corrales had a good excuse for bringing in a relief pitcher even though Kern said he wasn't tired:

"He told me, 'No, but the outfielders sure are.' "

...

When a team trainer asked Cal State–Fullerton defensive back Ron McLean why he was resting on the training table with his uniform on, McLean explained:

"The uniform needs rest, too."

...

Outfielder Bake McBride of the St. Louis Cardinals, on why he quit smoking:

"In spring training, there were too many doubles and triples to run out. I got tired of it all."

...

After admitting to illegal recruiting practices that resulted in a three-year probation for Clemson, the Tigers' former basketball coach Tates Locke explained why he did it:

"I got tired of losing."

THE TROTS

Hey, even horses know how to trot. Not always so with teams or an occasional home-run hitter. Perhaps they should watch some films of the best trotters racing in the famed Hambletonian. Well, it couldn't hurt!

... ...

Boston Celtics coach Tom Heinsohn, on the reasons for a loss to the New Orleans Jazz:

"We didn't play well tonight. Heck, we didn't even trot well."

...

Chicago White Sox catcher Jim Essian, on why he didn't use a home-run trot after bashing his first homer in 101 major-league games:

"I wanted to go into my home-run trot, but I realized I didn't have one."

...

Larry Bird—after missing most of the season with an injury—explaining why he would not make a brief playoff appearance as Dodger Kirk Gibson did when he hit a game-winning home run in the opener of the 1988 World Series:

"I don't have a home-run trot yet."

20
Eat, Drink, and ...
Exercise!

EATING ESCAPADES

Who doesn't like to eat? Some people will eat almost
anything. Others, however, are a little bit more picky
about their menu selections. Here are various excuses
and explanations for important decisions involving
food. Come and get it!

... ...

New York pitcher Catfish Hunter—whose diabetic
condition dictated that he carry candy with him—on
not carrying the candy bar named after Yankee Reggie
Jackson:

"I'm afraid I'd get mustard all over me."

...

Russ Grimm, Washington Redskins offensive lineman,
explaining his transition from a 6'3", 205-pound prep
quarterback to a 270-pound center for the University
of Pittsburgh:

"I ate my way onto the offensive line."

Archie Moore, ex–light heavyweight champion, responding to reports that he overeats:

"I am not a glutton, but I am an explorer of food."

...

Football color commentator John Madden, who starred in a noted beer commercial, on the reason he stopped smoking and began chewing cigars:

"They taste great, and they're less filling."

...

Baseball broadcaster Ralph Kiner got the following excuse from slugger Dick Allen for avoiding an appearance on Kiner's postgame show:

"He said if he came on, all the cold cuts would be gone when he got back to the locker room."

...

Buzzy Bavasi, San Diego Padres president, on his motivation for voting to keep the Giants in San Francisco during an attempted franchise shift in 1976:

"Well, it's close and they have all those fine restaurants."

...

Golfer Chi Chi Rodriguez, on why he eats red meat every day:

"They say red meat is bad for you, but I never saw a sick-looking tiger."

...

Three-hundred-pound Art Donovan, former Baltimore Colts defensive lineman, on the reason he calls himself a light eater:

"As soon as it's light, I start to eat."

...

Rocky Bridges, San Francisco Giants coach, on his refusal to eat snails:

"I prefer fast food."

BOTTOMS UP!

Alcohol has been around sports for years. Fans drink up before, during, and after games. Beer commercials pervade sports broadcasts. Team management must decide whether to allow alcohol in the locker room and on team flights. Players must decide whether to go out drinking and carousing with the boys after a game. So it naturally follows that the world of sports flows with excuses related to alcohol and drinking.

... ...

Golfer Lee Davis, on why he always seemed to struggle in the Pacific Coast Amateur tournament when it was held in Utah:

"I've never played well in Utah because you can't get a drink. You spend all your time standing in line for a Coke at Burger King."

...

Bobby Sheehan, NHL player with the Colorado Rockies, on why he claimed stories of his past drinking were exaggerated:

"It wasn't that I drank so much; it's just that I put it into such a small body."

...

Ruben Olivares, ex-bantamweight and -featherweight boxing champion, on whether he drinks:

"Only when I'm drunk."

...

Michel Lourie, French national sprint coach, on why France had failed to produce great track and field teams the way it produces great wines:

"Perhaps it is precisely because of our great wines that we have not had great track teams."

...

San Francisco Giants manager Frank Robinson, on the reason his team roster included so many older players:

"I have to have someone to drink with."

...

Former California Angels infielder Syd O'Brien, on why he became a liquor distributor:

"It was the closest thing to baseball I could find."

...

Former Detroit Lions quarterback Bobby Layne, after drinking a quart of Bloody Marys during a round of golf:

"My hope is to run out of money and breath at the same time."

THE EXERCISE QUOTIENT

Running, walking, aerobics . . . however you do it, the message is the same: "Get in shape!" But ever notice how everyone is an exercise expert today? Well, I guess if Jane Fonda did it, anyone can! Here are the excuses and opinions of some "experts" involving the exercise quotient.

... ...

New York Yankee pitcher Luis Tiant, on not running with the other pitchers:

"How many 20-game seasons has Jesse Owens got?"

...

Former pitcher Jim Kaat, citing a somewhat popular excuse for not believing in wind sprints:

"Jesse Owens never won a baseball game in his life."

...

Portland forward Maurice Lucas, after Trail Blazer coach Jack Ramsay admonished him for talking during stretching drills, on why he should be able to talk:

"Jack LaLanne talks during his stretching exercises."

...

Vasily Alexeyev, gold-medal heavyweight lifter for the Soviet Union in the 1976 Summer Olympics, on whether jogging was part of his training:

"No, I walk. The turtle only walks and he lives 300 years."

Joaquin Andujar, Oakland A's pitcher, on the reason he walked away from team stretching drills:

"Babe Ruth never stretched.'

...

Yogi Berra, excusing himself for not knowing his cap size during spring training:

"I'm not in shape yet."

...

Baseball Commissioner Bowie Kuhn, on why he had made jogging his new hobby:

"Normalcy has returned ... Owners again are chasing the commissioner."

...

Announcer Curt Gowdy, on one reason the athletes of today seem to have longer sports careers:

"Arabic exercises."

21
America's Pastime

PITCHING PURSUITS

Be a pitcher. Be in the spotlight. Be a hero if your team wins. But be a bum if you are tagged for that game-winning home run. Pitching is probably the most visible role in sports. Where else does a player get to work from higher ground than the rest of the players? No wonder the best pitchers get put on a pedestal! Here are some illuminating excuses and explanations involving the art of pitching.

... ...

When Louisville pitcher John Martin was shelled by Denver for seven runs in just two and two-thirds innings during an American Association contest, he offered two excuses:

> *"First, we flew American Airlines into Denver and we usually fly TWA. Second, there seemed to be an abundance of nimbus clouds in the area that seemed to make my knuckleball high."*

...

Philadelphia manager Danny Ozark, on why Phillies relief pitcher Ron Reed had just surrendered five consecutive hits:

"He was just throwing where the bat was going."

...

St. Louis Cardinals right-hander Rick Ownby, explaining his troubles on the mound:

"They want me to throw it over the plate and I can't pitch that way."

...

Jim Kaat, Philadelphia Phillies hurler, on the reason he pitches so rapidly:

"If the game lasts more than two hours, my pitches turn into pumpkins."

...

Chicago White Sox hurler Steve Stone, on why he decided to develop a forkball:

"The idea came from watching so many of my balls going out of the park."

...

New York Mets pitcher Harry Parker had this alibi after walking nine batters to equal Nolan Ryan's single-game team mark:

"Actually, my control wasn't that bad. I was just missing with pitches."

...

Detroit Tigers starting pitcher Walt Terrell, on the reason he took an early exit against the New York Yankees:

"I was so wild I would have walked Manute Bol four times."

...

Pittsburgh Pirates pitcher Dave LaPoint, explaining his eight-hit, three-walk effort in a 7–5 loss to the New York Mets:

"I made dumb pitches when I had to."

...

Jim Morrison, Atlanta Braves infielder, on how he accomplished his scoreless appearance as a reliever against San Francisco:

"Basically, I had things on my side because I know how stupid hitters are."

...

Toronto utility player Bob Bailor, after making a successful pitching debut by retiring all four Cleveland batters he faced, explaining his fastball:

"It would have been better, but it got caught up in the bugs between the mound and home plate."

...

Minnesota Twins pitcher Eddie Bane, on his mound skills:

"I think I throw the ball as hard as anyone. The ball just doesn't get there as fast."

...

Chicago White Sox reliever Ricky Horton, explaining his high 5.90 ERA:

"I'm a finesse pitcher with no finesse."

...

New York Yankees pitcher Tommy John, on giving up consecutive, run-scoring singles against Kansas City:

"I can only throw them; I can't direct them."

...

Los Angeles Angels hurler Bo Belinsky, attempting to excuse his poor pitching performance in a 15–0 loss in 1963:

"How can a guy win a game if you don't give him any runs?"

SPITTERS, DROOLERS, AND GREASEBALLS

Baseball has always been the main arena for spitters. There are the players with their chaws of tobacco who need to squirt out the juice periodically. Then, of course, there are all those pitchers who flirt with throwing the spitter in some form or another. To spit or not to spit? Even a football player was faced with that decision in the early days of artificial turf. Here are excuses and explanations related to the spit-and-polish side of sports.

... ...

Blanche Perry, wife of famed spitball pitcher Gaylord Perry, on why she often makes errant throws while playing catch with her husband during the off-season:

"It's because the ball is wet and hard to grip."

...

Hall of Famer Johnny Bench, after recording a double-, triple-, and quintuple-bogey during the Cincinnati Metropolitan Amateur Golf Championship:

"Gaylord Perry had the only thing harder to hit than a golf ball."

...

Hall of Famer pitcher Early Wynn, on why he never experimented with throwing the spitter:

"My philosophy was that the ball was made of horsehide then and any horse I was going to kiss, I'd have to know real well first."

...

Willard Harrell, rookie running back for the Green Bay Packers, on the reason he preferred not to play on artificial turf:

"Sometimes during a game I have to spit, but I can't do it on artificial turf. I feel like I'm spitting on the carpet."

...

Lew Burdette, Atlanta pitching coach and a three-game winner in the 1958 World Series for Milwaukee, on how the Braves were hitting his famed spitter during batting practice:

"I've slowed down so much, they're hitting the dry side."

New York Yankees catcher Rick Cerone, on why he employed a spitter when called upon as an emergency reliever during a 20–3 loss to the Texas Rangers:

"I didn't have my good stuff."

...

Chicago Cubs relief pitcher George Frazier, making a qualified admission that he had thrown spitters and doctored pitches:

"I don't put any foreign substance on the base-ball. Everything I use on it is from the good ol' U.S.A."

STRIKEOUTS, WHIFFS, AND K'S

An unwritten baseball rule is that those who whiff are obligated to explain it to reduce their embarrassment. After all, nobody likes to strike out! A player may tell teammates something like, "He's got nothing; he's throwing junk." Or, if caught looking at strike three, the player can say, "That wasn't even close. The ump blew it." And if recording a "K" by going down swinging at a Nolan Ryan fastball, the player can simply explain, "How can you hit something you can't see!"

... ...

Cesar Geronimo, former major leaguer, on going into the record book as the 3,000th strikeout victim of both Nolan Ryan and Bob Gibson:

"I was just in the right place at the right time."

...

Darryl Strawberry, New York Mets outfielder, on why umpire Terry Tata ejected him for disputing a called third strike during a long, extra-inning night game:

"He said the strike zone changes at 3:00 A.M."

...

Hall of Fame pitcher Bob Feller, explaining how he whiffed Willie Mays in a spring training Old-Timers Game:

> *"I threw Mays nothing, and he was looking for something."*

...

California Angels infielder Billy Grabarkewitz, who made that long walk back to the dugout often in his career, on why he seldom struck out early in the season:

> *"I'm a slow starter."*

...

New York Yankee Reggie Jackson—part of a classic ninth-inning confrontation in Game 2 of the 1978 World Series—with his alibi for whiffing on a 3-and-2 pitch with two on and two out against Los Angeles rookie pitcher Bob Welch in the Dodgers' 4-3 win:

> *"I was thinking so much about getting the bat on the baseball that I neglected to associate that the runners always move on a 3–2 pitch with two out. I picked up Bucky Dent running. I lost sight of the ball."*

...

Cleveland Indians outfielder Benny Ayala, expressing his frustration at being nailed with a called third strike despite the 2-ball and 1-strike count shown on the scoreboard before the pitch:

> *"You can't trust anything these days."*

THAT SLUMPING FEELING

Say the word "slump" and one thinks baseball. Hitting 90-m.p.h. fastballs and wicked curves isn't exactly the easiest skill to learn in the world. So, even the game's top players get their opportunity to be mired in a slump. Here are some explanations and excuses by players with that slumping feeling.

... ...

Davey Lopes, second baseman for the Los Angeles Dodgers, on why he had gone hitless in his past 25 at-bats to drop his batting average below .100:

"I'm trying to get down to zero and start the season over."

...

California Angels infielder Billy Grabarkewitz, trying to put his .150 batting average into perspective:

"I'm hitting so bad I could go into a slump and raise my average."

...

Frank Feneck, Tiger Stadium's assistant director of operations, on the most popular excuse used by players to explain a batting slump:

"When a guy gets in a slump he always blames it on the field."

...

Rusty Staub, on the reason he was only hitting .219 at home for the Detroit Tigers:

"Tiger Stadium has the worst infield I've ever seen. The last homestand, it cost me seven hits."

Baseball Commissioner Ford Frick, attempting to explain during one season why major-league attendance was slumping:

"We anticipated this leveling off after five straight seasons of rising attendances."

LIVELY-BALL SYNDROME

Baseball seems to experience the mysterious "home-run glut" every few seasons. What causes this phenomenon? Is the ball actually livelier during those seasons or do pitchers experience some form of mass hurler hallucination? Whatever the reasons, the lively-ball syndrome, besides giving rise to various hypotheses, makes a popular alibi for pitchers tagged for home runs.

... ...

Phil Garner, infielder for the Houston Astros, on the cause for a home-run glut during the 1987 season:

"With the decrease in ozone layers, we've lost some of the ionized particles, so there's nothing to hold those balls back."

...

Chicago White Sox coach Eddie Brinkman, on the same glut:

"There's a hole in the ozone layer."

...

Cleveland Indians pitching coach Jack Aker, on the reason for the 1987 home-run bonanza:

"It's the underground testing. Gravity is leaving the earth and so are the baseballs."

Chicago Cubs pitcher Rick Sutcliffe, on whether the baseball was livelier in 1987 than in other seasons:

"I think pitchers needed an excuse. Every now and then you have to give the hitters credit. I pitched in Wrigley Field. You could hit a tomato out of there."

...

Detroit Tigers manager Sparky Anderson, on why his team was able to smash six homers in one game during the 1986 season:

"The ball has special ingredients. Elements from outer space."

...

Oakland A's pitcher Rick Langford, after being tagged for three homers and 11 hits in a 6–4 loss during the 1982 season:

"I'm not using this as an excuse, but they're using a livelier ball this year."

...

Greg Gross of the Chicago Cubs, asked to ponder whether a lively ball was being used during the 1977 season:

"When you only get one home run every six years, there's no such thing as a lively ball."

...

Milwaukee Brewers pitcher Jim Slaton, asked during the 1977 season if the ball was livelier than in past seasons:

"Only when I'm pitching."

GOING, GOING, GONE!

The home run is one of the most exciting moments in sports. Of course, pitchers have to make excuses for giving up the long ball. Banjo hitters must alibi for not hitting any at all and when they do happen to hit one, they must somehow explain that, too.

··· ··· ···

Infielder Mick Kelleher, with his alibi for going homerless in 10 major-league seasons with Detroit and California:

"What's one home run? If you hit one, they are just going to want you to hit two."

···

Texas Rangers outfielder Mickey Rivers, who had hit only one home run in each of the two previous seasons, explaining his latest blast, which barely cleared the fence:

"I've been working on my golf game and I guess that was the cause of my homer."

···

Announcer Steve Blass, on the reason the Pittsburgh Pirates and Chicago Cubs had smashed six homers during a contest at Wrigley Field:

"The air must be corked."

···

Mel Hall of the Cleveland Indians, excusing himself for failing to yet hit a home run two months into the season:

"I'm waiting for the father-son game."

Ron Darling of the New York Mets, offering an explanation of his home-run pitch to Houston's Alan Ashby:

"It was a split-finger fastball that didn't split."

...

Pittsburgh Pirates pitcher John Candelaria, on getting tagged for a lot of home runs:

"I throw a lot of strikes."

22
See the World

GOING MY WAY?

Hey, jocks, wouldn't it be fantastic to hold every competition at home! Dream on! Pack that suitcase and get aboard that plane, bus, train, or pack mule for your next voyage to enemy turf. How do they do it? Here are some insights into the traveling life.

....

Cleveland coach Marty Schottenheimer, on the reason the Browns would take a plane instead of a bus—their usual mode of travel to games at Pittsburgh:

"I always get nosebleeds on buses."

...

Vanderbilt basketball coach C. M. Newton, on his habit of always sitting in the last seat during team flights:

"I've never heard of a plane that backed into a mountain."

...

Boston general manager Jan Volk, explaining the absence of Celtic center Robert Parish from the team's summer Caribbean cruise:

"Robert doesn't do boats."

...

Air Force football coach Ben Martin, explaining his decision to use United Airlines for the Falcons' team flights:

"I don't trust those Air Force planes."

...

Nate Branch, Harlem Globetrotters player-coach, on the reason the team's travel schedule wasn't too bad:

"We only have one road trip a year."

...

Dubuque College football coach Don Turner, after his team was beaten on the road by Wisconsin-Platteville, 49–7:

"Our best drive of the evening was the 25-mile trip to Platteville."

...

Center Joe Barry Carroll, on leaving the Golden State Warriors to play in the Italian basketball league for Simac of Milan:

"I had never been in Italy, and I think it can be useful to me—visiting an unknown part of the world."

...

Pro bowler Mark Williams, on why he uses a van for his travels on the Professional Bowlers' Association (PBA) tour:

"I'd sure like to fly, but did you ever try to check 20 bowling balls?"

...

Quarterback Eddie LeBaron of the Dallas Cowboys, during the franchise's early days, on the reason for his premature departure from a luncheon:

"A man just called from Amarillo and wants to buy four season tickets. I'm flying them to him."

...

Montreal manager Gene Mauch, on why the Expos were chancing a late afternoon departure from Chicago for a night game in Philadelphia against Cy Young Award-winner Steve Carlton:

"When Steve Carlton is pitching, you look for any excuse to miss a game."

HOME/ROAD

Take your pick: "There's no place like home" or "Hit the road, Jack!" Here are some excuses and explanations about the differences between playing at home and on the road.

... ...

Arkansas football coach Lou Holtz, on why playing road games did not bother him:

"I play as well on the road as I do at home, but my teams don't."

...

Light heavyweight boxer Bill Marsh, after being kayoed in Kansas City, Kansas, by a hometown fighter, on why he had only a 4–11 record for the year:

"Mostly, I've been fighting in everybody's hometown."

Philadelphia Phillies manager Danny Ozark, explaining the impact of managerial decisions on a team's play:

> *"It's most important at home, because you play more games there."*

...

Ex-Detroit Red Wings coach Harry Neale, on the team's poor home and road records during his last season at the helm:

> *"My failure was that I couldn't think of anyplace else to play."*

...

Oakland coach John Madden, on why he was not counting up the victories just because the Raiders had four of their next five games at home:

> *"I never heard of a stadium winning a football game."*

...

Los Angeles Lakers center Mychal Thompson, on the reason the team is much more successful at home in Southern California than on the road:

> *"We're a lot more comfortable breathing air that we can see."*

...

Detroit Tigers manager Ralph Houk, explaining losing streaks:

> *"When you get in a slump on the road, the best thing to do is to get home. When you get in a slump at home, the best thing is to get on the road."*

MELTING-POT HERITAGE

America, the great melting pot. Our diversity of nationalities gives Americans much familiarity with other peoples and races. That understanding comes in handy for those trying to utilize explanations involving heritage.

... ...

University of Texas basketball coach Abe Lemons, explaining what it's like to be part Indian:

"Believe me, there are drawbacks. Every time I dance, it rains."

...

Notre Dame football coach Ara Parseghian, explaining his handicap to a golfer:

"I'm half Armenian."

...

Muhammad Ali, during a visit to Italy, on the difference between Italians in the United States and Italians in Italy:

"There are a lot more of them in Italy."

...

NFL quarterback great, Norm Van Brocklin, on why God created whiskey:

"To keep the Irish from ruling the world."

...

Arizona State football coach Frank Kush, explaining what it would take to defeat Fiesta Bowl opponent Missouri:

"This probably sounds like a Polish philosophy, but we're going to have to score more than they do."

23
The Mass Media

TELEVISION AND FILM: THAT'S A WRAP!

Okay, so television basically controls sports. That means the overlapping of formerly separated sports seasons: World Series games occurring in cold weather, hockey's Stanley Cup decided in late spring's warm weather, the NBA basketball playoffs going on for an eternity, and the airing of what seems like 20 college football games every Saturday. So, naturally, excuses develop involving the television and video age. Here is a choice selection.

... ...

Former Boston Bruins coach Don Cherry, explaining why hockey teams don't conduct evening practice sessions to get in sync with their games, which are played at night:

> *"I don't think the players would like missing* 'Starsky and Hutch.'"

...

Lee Roy Selmon, Tampa Bay defensive end, excusing himself for not knowing how he did in his first football game with Eufaula Junior High in Oklahoma:

"I haven't seen the films."

Chicago Bears running back Walter Payton, on why he doesn't watch "Monday Night Football":

"It makes as much sense as a secretary going home and spending her nights typing."

...

George Foreman, making a boxing comeback, on the reason it took him seven rounds to defeat Dwight Muhammad Qawi in a televised bout:

"They've got commercials to put in. I can't send everyone home early."

...

Boxing manager David Wolf, on why the next three bouts of his boxer Ed "Too Tall" Jones—who was taking a year off from the Dallas Cowboys—wouldn't be televised as were his earlier fights:

"We don't want Ed to be a captive of the networks."

...

Chicago Bears placekicker Bob Thomas, on the reason he claimed he once made a field goal by deliberately kicking the ball off the crossbar so that it fell over for three points:

"When I kick them through the uprights, I never get on the 10 o'clock news."

...

Jerome Brown, Philadelphia Eagles rookie defensive tackle, gives this alibi for being chased down and tackled from behind by Herschel Walker of the Dallas Cowboys while running with a recovered fumble:

"I was watching myself on the stadium monitor."

...

Minnesota Vikings coach Bud Grant, on why he always appeared unemotional when the TV cameras panned him standing on the sidelines:

"Television has those directors. Whenever they see Hank Stram pacing the sidelines they say 'Get him.' When they see George Allen cheerleading they say 'Get him.' And when they see me standing still they say 'Get him.'"

...

Mike Johnson, UC–Davis defensive back, on how television caused the team to allow 16 first-quarter points en route to a 39–30 loss to Lehigh:

"We were just thinking about how wonderful it was being on national TV for the first time that we didn't concentrate like we should have."

...

Executive director Ed Garvey of the NFL Players Association, on the effectiveness of picket lines during a players' strike against the NFL:

"We won't be able to tell until we study the films."

...

Television color analyst Bill Robertson, on why the Titan Cable Sports network's broadcast of the Cal State–Fullerton—Nevada-Reno football game left the air after three quarters:

"They hired a Vietnamese student as a technician, and he thought football games only had three quarters."

...

Cleveland coach Sam Rutigliano, on not running film of the Browns' 47–24 loss to Seattle:

"I don't believe in showing pornographic movies."

...

Former NFL quarterback and coach Norm Van Brocklin, on why football was getting high television ratings:

"Everything else on TV is so bad."

DON'T QUOTE ME ON THAT

Where would sports be without media coverage? Well, athletes' salaries would be a lot smaller! Despite this fact, athletes and coaches sometimes resent it when sportswriters point out their mistakes. Then they criticize sportswriters for not having actually played the game—implying that writers don't really know the game at all. These same Neanderthals probably think reporters covering the White House must have served in high office or that business reporters must have been employed by General Motors or IBM! Here are some insightful explanations involving reporters.

... ...

Cliff Temple, British track and field writer, offering his analysis of sportswriters:

"A [sports] journalist is someone who would if he could, but he can't, so he tells those who already can how they should."

...

Oakland Raiders coach John Madden, on why he didn't know who his starting quarterback would be two weeks before the opener:

"Hell, if I was smart enough to know what I'd do two weeks from now, I'd be smart enough to be a sportswriter."

...

St. Louis Cardinal Pedro Guerrero, explaining his pet peeve in dealing with sportswriters:

"Sometimes they write what I say and not what I mean."

...

Sparky Anderson, moving into the broadcasting booth after being fired as Cincinnati Reds manager, on how he got players to talk so freely during interviews:

"I learned when I was on the other end not to ask stupid questions."

...

Pee Wee Reese, former Brooklyn Dodger shortstop and ex–national television broadcaster, on his method for always getting along with the media:

"I never read the papers after we lost a game."

PROMOTIONAL ACTIVITIES

A promotional effort usually begins with a simple idea. Sometimes that brainstorm works great. Sometimes that idea is limited because there's nothing great to promote. Other times the idea works for awhile and then grows stale. Nobody ever said promoting something was easy!

Pete Rose, alias "Charlie Hustle," on the reason he slides head first:

"It's the fastest way to get to the base, it is probably the safest, and it usually gets my picture in the paper."

...

David Courtney, public relations director for the Los Angeles Kings, explaining why he wouldn't be putting together a highlights film after the team had a lackluster season:

"What we have is a highlights slide."

...

Atlanta Chiefs vice president Terry Hanson, on why gimmicks to draw fans to games of the struggling North American Soccer League were no longer successful:

"You can only bring the players in on the back of a fire truck so many times."

THERE'S NO BUSINESS LIKE SHOW BUSINESS

Fans want to be entertained, and what better way to do it than with show biz! But sometimes it takes a lot more than a juggling act or team mascot to entertain. It takes crazy men! Here are two examples of show business in sports.

... ...

Former major-league owner Bill Veeck, on the reason he didn't pay a high-wire walker who fell at a game:

"Look, the guy fell behind the scoreboard where no one could see him. Any showman would have fallen in front of the scoreboard."

...

Patrick O'Brien, alias "Captain Dynamite," on why at the age of 60 he continued his Demolition Derby circuit act—where he crawls into a dynamite-lined coffin and blows himself up:

"Show biz sort of gets in your blood."

24
It All
Balances Out

LEFT/RIGHT

No, this category isn't about radicals versus conservatives. This is much bigger than that! It's about right-handers versus left-handers. Everyone knows it's primarily a right-handed world. But the sports world offers equal opportunity for both sides. Here are some excuses and explanations for things left and right.

... ...

ABC sports announcer Al Michaels, on his assessment of switch-hitting third baseman Bobby Bonilla of the Pittsburgh Pirates:

"He's a better interview from the left side than from the right side."

...

Pro golfer Bob Menne, explaining his lack of success at hitting drives straight down the middle of the fairway:

"I'm playing military golf—left, right, left, right, left, right..."

Duffy Daugherty, television analyst and former Michigan State coach, upon seeing right-handed quarterback Cornelius Greene of Ohio State fling a left-handed desperation pass:

"Not only is he ambidextrous but he can throw with either hand."

...

Kansas City Royals manager Jack McKeon, explaining why .218 was his highest batting average during a minor-league career as a catcher:

"I was one of the few guys in baseball who could hit three ways—left, right, and seldom."

...

Houston Oilers rookie quarterback Dan Pastorini, who throws right-handed and does everything else left-handed, with one exception:

"I eat spaghetti with both hands."

...

Rookie pro golfer Jim Nelford, on why he drives righty and putts lefty:

"My dad was left-handed and my mother right-handed. I borrowed whichever set of clubs was available."

...

Joe Yamin, a switch-hitting outfielder with the Pewter Mug Tavern softball team in Watervliet, New York, on the reason he didn't hit right-handed after whiffing left-handed three times on just nine pitches:

"I can't hit with power right-handed."

...

Race-car owner Roger Penske has his alibi for why his 18th-hole drive at Pebble Beach hooked left and splashed into Carmel Bay during the Bing Crosby Pro-Am:

"What do you expect? Race drivers are used to turning left all the time."

...

Southpaw pitcher Bill Lee of the Montreal Expos, on why he didn't regard himself a flake:

"Flake is a right-handed term."

...

Cleveland coach Sam Rutigliano, on whether Seattle Seahawks quarterback Jim Zorn caused problems for the Browns' defensive secondary because he is a left-hander:

"No, all four of my defensive backs are right-handed hitters."

...

Left-hander Woody Hayes, on the cause of five interceptions thrown by right-handed Ohio State freshman quarterback Art Schlichter in a 19–0 loss to Penn State:

"He was throwing the ball with the wrong arm."

...

Pittsburgh Pirates star Willie Stargell, explaining to a young fan why his Rolls-Royce has the steering wheel on the "wrong" side:

"Because I'm left-handed."

...

Detroit Pistons forward Kelly Tripucka, on the reason he possesses a propensity for left-handed dunks:

"My left arm is longer."

...

Luis Gonzalez, first baseman for the University of South Alabama, on his NCAA record of being hit by a pitch for the 33rd time in two years:

"I guess I'm just one of those people who is always in the right place at the right time."

LIKES AND DISLIKES

Someone without likes or dislikes is . . . boring! Ask someone to expound on his or her likes and dislikes in life and the conversation might go on for hours. Offered here are some insightful explanations and excuses for the likes and dislikes of those in sports.

... ...

Cincinnati Reds manager Sparky Anderson, on the reason he liked his new bubble-gum baseball card:

"They've taken my playing record off and put my managerial record on."

...

Air Force football coach Ben Martin, on why he isn't a proponent of large coaching staffs:

"I don't want coaches coaching coaches."

...

Tom Mack, offensive guard for the Los Angeles Rams, on the reason he liked to lead the sweep:

"Well, after bashing my head against 290-pound defensive linemen all day, there's nothing more exciting than to turn the corner and see a 180-pound cornerman in front of me."

...

Boxer Jim Winfield, kayoed by Bobo Renfrow in the first round, on why kneeling on one knee was as far as he got up after being knocked down:

>*"I don't like the sight of blood. That's why I didn't get up."*

...

Alabama football coach Bear Bryant, on why he liked employing the wishbone offense:

>*"The reason I like it so much is we've been winning with it."*

...

USC football coach John McKay, explaining why he doesn't like his players jumping up and down before the kickoff:

>*"All that means is somebody could jump on the coach's feet."*

...

Retired basketball star Julius "Dr. J" Erving, on his preference for playing golf instead of basketball with his three sons and one daughter:

>*"When we play basketball, all I get to do is rebound because all my kids want to do is shoot."*

...

ESPN analyst Beano Cook, on why flying isn't one of his favorite things in life:

>*"The first word you see in every airport is* termi-nal.*"*

...

New York Jets running back John Riggins, on the reason he likes pro football:

"You've got to like a job where you don't go to work until noon."

...

Montreal Expos pitcher Bill Lee, offering an explanation for the cause of strife between managers and pitchers:

"Most of the managers are lifetime .220 hitters. For years, pitchers have been getting these managers out 75 percent of the time, and that's why they don't like us."

...

San Francisco Giants manager Bill Rigney, on their paucity of runs:

"We've got good hitters . . . but they like to hit singles."

...

Ivan Lendl, on why he dislikes playing night tennis matches:

"I think night is for dinner, bed, and watching hockey games."

...

HBO sportscaster Barry Thompkins, on why he likes covering tennis more than boxing:

"Nobody ever bleeds on your tuxedo."

...

World-class sprinter Steve Williams, on his motivation for skipping an indoor meet during the 1970s between the United States and Soviet Union in Leningrad:

"I'd rather be around happy people."

LOST AND FOUND

Remember the last time you misplaced something or got lost and couldn't find the object or your destination right away? Athletes also are involved in similar episodes. Here, they try to excuse or explain them.

... ...

After Miami Dolphins fullback Larry Csonka rushed for 102 yards in a game, he was asked in the locker room if he had set any goals:

"Well, yes. At the moment I'd like to find my socks."

...

Cincinnati Reds outfielder Dan Driessen—missing for several days after his sudden departure from a Puerto Rican winter baseball league—offered an explanation upon being found in Hilton Head, South Carolina:

"I'm not missing. I know where I am."

...

Golfer Tom Watson, on how he helped the golf game of former president Gerald Ford:

"First, hitting the ball. Second, finding where it went."

...

When San Diego manager Dick Williams went to the mound and asked for the ball after Padres pitcher Tim Lollar was tagged for a Mike Schmidt home run, Williams received this explanation:

"He said it was in the second level, about eight rows up."

...

Lightweight boxing champion Alexis Arguello, asked by his son what he was doing on the canvas after Andy Ganijan knocked him down during a bout:

"I was down there looking for my pride."

...

PGA golfer Tony Lema, on why he spent several days at Arnold Palmer's house:

"I got lost in the vault."

THE GOOD, THE BAD, AND THE UGLY

"Hey, I'm good, he's bad, and you're ugly!" Well, we are what we are. After all, it takes all kinds in sports. Just remember that these types of judgments are in the eye of the beholder and often balance out over time. You may be good today, bad tomorrow, and ugly next week. Here are some good, bad, and ugly excuses, alibis, and explanations.

... ...

Olympic gold-medalist Frank Shorter, on the reason he runs marathons:

"Because I'm good at it."

Wally Hilgenberg, Minnesota Vikings linebacker, explaining his exhibition wrestling match with a 550-pound bear named Victor:

"It was a bit like wrestling some of the tight ends around the NFL, except the bear's breath was worse."

...

Pete Rose, on why he wasn't over-the-hill yet at the age of 38:

"I don't have the average 38-year-old's body. I know my face looks old but if you'd slid head-first for 16 years, you'd be ugly, too."

...

When quick-witted, former 11-year major leaguer Rocky Bridges made his managerial debut by going down to the minors to direct the San Jose Bees, he was prepared with a good alibi:

"I managed good but, boy, did they play bad!"

...

Cincinnati Reds manager Sparky Anderson, on why his players don't join in singing the national anthem:

"Most of us have such bad voices we respect the national anthem by not singing it."

...

When Arizona State quarterback Dennis Sproul arrived at practice sporting shoulder-length hair, Sun Devils football coach Frank Kush told him:

"It looks real nice. But I don't want nice-looking quarterbacks. I want an ugly one who completes passes."

Buzzy Bavasi, president of the lowly San Diego Padres, after reports of a proposed sale that would keep the franchise in San Diego:

"The good news is that we may stay here and the bad news, I guess, is the same thing."

...

When Chicago Cubs rookie pitcher Bill Bonham failed to retire the four St. Louis Cardinals hitters he faced in his major-league debut he explained:

"I guess I was due for a bad outing."

...

Chicago coach Jack Pardee, explaining the Bears' embarrassing 35–7 trouncing at the hands of the Baltimore Colts:

"When we got to our dressing room before the game, we found six inches of sewage from backed-up pipes, so we went out there and stunk up the field."

...

Earl Campbell, star running back for the Houston Oilers, after walking out on a pro-am team at the Houston Open golf tournament:

"It was too hot, and I wasn't doin' any good no way."

...

All-time golfing great Sam Snead, on the damage a balky putter can cause:

"A bad putter is like a bad apple in a barrel. First, it turns your chipping game sour. Then it begins to eat into your irons, and finally, it just cleans the head off your driver."

...

New Orleans coach Bum Phillips, on taking his wife with him on the road:

"I usually take my wife with me on trips because she's too ugly to kiss goodbye."

25
Out of the Heavens

RELIGIOUS REVELATIONS

The question of God and sports often arises in today's sports world. There are those athletes who publicly praise God when they win, but somehow neglect to publicly praise Him when they lose. Does God really care who wins or loses? Since religion does pop up in sports, here are some religious explanations and excuses that may be revealing. And you don't even have to take them on faith!

... ...

The Reverend John Durkin—after teaming with pro golfer Lou Graham to win a pro-am competition—on whether he was responsible for the tournament's perfect weather:

"No, that's management. I'm sales."

...

Atlanta Braves catcher Gene Oliver, on why he was hitting a miraculous .415 against Sandy Koufax:

"He thinks I'm Jewish."

Wake Forest basketball coach Jack McCloskey, explaining religion's impact, after his team was beaten by St. Joseph's of Philadelphia:

"I don't mind when we play a Catholic school and the referee is Catholic, but when the game is on Ash Wednesday and the ref shows up with a smudge on his forehead, I know I'm in trouble."

...

Ohio State quarterback Cornelius Greene, on why he had taken up reading the Bible:

"When you play quarterback for Woody Hayes, you need all the faith you can get."

...

Lee Trevino, who once was hit by lightning during a tournament, on the reason he grabs his one-iron and holds it overhead when he sees lightning on a golf course:

"Because even the Good Lord has trouble hitting a one-iron."

...

Of course, Trevino leaves himself another option. Why does he have a Plan B of getting off the golf course as soon as there is an approaching storm?:

"When God wants to play through, you let Him play through."

...

Houston Astros shortstop Roger Metzger, on his humble .088 batting average early in the season:

"I think I've figured out why I start so slow at the plate every year. I've been giving up hitting for Lent."

...

Richard Roberts, Oral Roberts University executive vice president, on the connection between his religion and his hopes for the school's basketball squad:

"I don't expect us to go 28–0, but I don't believe you can be a witness for Christ and go 0–28."

...

ABC publicist Beano Cook, on the network's decision to program a Notre Dame–Michigan State football game against the major-league baseball playoffs:

"We figure there are more Catholics than baseball fans."

...

The Reverend Billy Graham, on whether praying helps his golf game:

"Prayer never seems to work for me on the golf course. I think it has something to do with my being a terrible putter."

...

Oakland A's manager Alvin Dark, explaining the relationship between his religion and sportswriters:

"The Lord taught me to love everybody. But the last ones the Lord taught me to love were the sportswriters."

Columbia basketball coach Wayne Szoke, before his Lions lost by 19 points to No. 1-ranked St. John's, a Catholic university:

"It's a case of the Lions being thrown to the Christians."

...

Eddie Edwards, Cincinnati Bengals defensive end, on why he thought divine intervention was involved when Pittsburgh's Matt Bahr missed a last-second, potential game-winning field goal:

"I was praying too hard. I think that's why he missed it."

...

Seattle Mariners second baseman Harold Reynolds, on his religious reasons for switching from jersey number 37 to number 19:

"One of my favorite Bible verses is Joshua 1:9."

...

Lee Trevino, after shanking an iron shot during a golf exhibition:

"That's my Oral Roberts–Billy Graham shot . . . the heeler."

RAINDROPS KEEP FALLIN' ON MY HEAD

Everybody gets a little wet when stormy weather hits. Of course, the weather also results in some offbeat excuses and explanations. Blaming bad weather for human woes goes back to antiquity. If you can't blame the weather, what can you blame?

... ...

Dave White, Rensselaer Polytechnic Institute football coach, explaining his coaching maneuvers during a downpour featuring thunder and lightning:

"I moved whenever the chains came near me and I tried to stay away from the taller players."

New York Jets coach Ken Shipp, recalling his days as a University of Miami assistant, on why he didn't retrieve a Hurricanes player who went outside to look at a real hurricane:

"There was no way I was going out in that storm after him. Besides, the kid wasn't even a regular."

...

Oklahoma football coach Barry Switzer, after a 49–0 rout of Colorado in a downpour that flooded the field, on the reason he couldn't coax some of his substitutes to play:

"They said they couldn't swim."

...

Joe Paterno, Penn State football coach, explaining why he refused to pin a 7–6 loss to Maryland on a driving rain:

"It rained on both sides of the field. At least, I think it did."

GONE WITH THE WIND

Blame it on the ol' wind! In places like Candlestick Park or Wrigley Field that might not be such a bad idea. It's funny how athletes don't blame really adverse conditions—such as a heavy snowfall, oppressive heat, or bitter cold—for their misplays or losses. The conditions were the same for both sides, they say. Doesn't the same go with the wind? Here are some rather blustery excuses.

... ...

San Francisco Giant pitcher Roger Mason—after a game in the infamous Candlestick Park wind tunnel—on why his apparent right-field single turned into an out at first base by Chicago Cubs outfielder Andre Dawson:

"I was running into the wind."

...

San Francisco Giants outfielder Larry Herndon, on why a ball went through his legs for an error during a game at Candlestick Park:

"I have a large glove and it's very loose. The winds swirl out there and they closed my glove."

...

Utility player Harry Spilman of the San Francisco Giants, with his alibi for going without a triple in nearly 700 plate appearances—including numerous at-bats at Candlestick Park:

"Every time I hit a ball that might be a triple, I'm running against the wind."

...

Spilman's San Francisco teammate Chris Speier, offering the former Houston Astro a windy excuse for his lack of triples with that team:

"What was your excuse when you played at the Astrodome? Running against the air-conditioning?"

...

Tampa Bay Buccaneers coach John McKay, on the failure of his team to score after getting inside the opponent's 15-yard line five times:

"We couldn't score against a strong wind."

...

St. Louis Cardinals outfielder Andy Van Slyke, on why he couldn't quite nab a home-run ball hit by Los Angeles slugger Mike Marshall at Dodger Stadium:

"It got up in the Sandinista winds."

...

Texas Rangers outfielder Mickey Rivers, on the difficult weather conditions during a home game at Arlington:

"Man, it was tough. The wind was blowing about 100 degrees."

Epilogue:
The Final Word

Where else but in sports could one find such a diversity of imaginative excuses, alibis, and explanations? Maybe that's part of our own excuse for enjoying sports so much. You never know what they'll come up with next! But next time you start making alibis for your favorite player, team, or your own athletic ineptitudes, remember this final word on excuses from Los Angeles Lakers coach Pat Riley:

"There's no such thing as coulda, shoulda, and woulda. If you shoulda and coulda, you woulda done it."

Index

Barfield, Jesse, 126
Barkley, Charles, 12, 117
Barnes, Marvin, 117
Bartee, Kyle, 139
Bavasi, Buzzy, 215, 259
Bayi, Filbert, 49
Beard, Butch, 63
Beck, Barry, 81, 135
Becker, Boris, 144
Belinsky, Bo, 224
Bell, Buddy, 70
Bench, Johnny, 225
Bennett, Winston, 190
Bennett, Carl, 152
Berra, Yogi, 10, 18, 33, 38, 67, 220
Berry, Raymond, 169
Bevacqua, Kurt, 25
Billingham, Jack, 97
Bingham, Rhonda, 90
Bird, Larry, 54, 202, 213
Birdsong, Otis, 33
Blab, Uwe, 104
Blanda, George, 7, 140
Blass, Steve, 232
Bliss, Dave, 113
Blue, Vida, 135
Blyleven, Bert, 128
Bochy, Bruce, 85
Bogue, Doug, 128
Bogues, Muggsy, 132
Bol, Manute, 168, 171, 177
Bombeck, Erma, 77
Bonds, Bobby, 61
Bonham, Bill, 259
Bonilla, Bobby, 249
Bosworth, Brian, 46
Bowa, Larry, 204
Bowden, Bobby, 77, 98
Boyd, Bob, 152

Boyd, Dennis "Oil Can," 23
Bradley, Pat, 150
Bradshaw, Terry, 205
Bragan, Bobby, 139
Branch, Nate, 235
Brannon, Buster, 56
Braverman, Al, 123
Breeden, Louis, 211
Breen, John, 77
Brett, George, 200
Bridges, Rocky, 47, 84, 216, 258
Brinkman, Eddie, 230
Brodie, John, 124
Brown, Dale, 113
Brown, Jerome, 243
Brown, Joe, 197
Brown, Larry, 63, 188, 204
Brown, Roosevelt, 80
Broyles, Frank, 30, 169
Bryant, Bear, 96, 254
Bryant, Ron, 48
Buckwalter, Morris "Bucky," 24
Buechler, Dick, 98
Burdette, Lew, 225
Burkhart, Ken, 200
Burleson, Tom, 177
Burns, Frank, 106
Butkus, Dick, 68
Byrd, Richard, 195

Camacho, Ernie, 205
Campanis, Al, 38
Campbell, Earl, 133, 152, 183, 259
Campbell, Robin, 104
Candelaria, John, 233
Cannell, Paul, 65
Canterbury, Tommy, 11, 59

Carey, Hugh, 125
Carlton, Steve, 199, 237
Carlyle, Randy, 187
Carman, Don, 198
Carner, JoAnne, 16
Carril, Pete, 4
Carroll, Barry, 235
Carroll, Clay, 79, 82
Carter, Harold, 167
Carter, Pancho, 127
Casanova, Tom, 76
Casper, Billy, 175, 205
Castillo, Marty, 205
Castillo, Zip, 49
Catlett, Gale, 119
Caudill, Bill, 43
Cauthen, Steve, 85
Cerone, Rick, 226
Chamberlain, Wilt, 81
Chandler, Bob, 120
Chang, Michael, 6
Charles, Russel, 156
Cherry, Don, 102, 241
Cias, Darryl, 48
Clampett, Bob, 171
Clark, Monte, 37
Clary, Ellis, 204
Cobb, Ty, 68
Cody, Wayne, 180
Colbert, Jim, 123
Cole, Larry, 8
Coleman, Jerry, 139
Collins, Dave, 202
Commings, Bob, 94, 97
Connors, Jimmy, 3, 5, 96
Conover, Al, 119
Cook, Beano, 151, 254, 263
Cook, Betty, 37
Cooke, Jack Kent, 99

Cooney, Gerry, 84
Cornelius, Ron, 196
Corrales, Pat, 134, 206, 212
Corso, Lee, 21, 31, 76, 134
Cosell, Howard, 130, 138
Cottier, Chuck, 9
Court, Margaret, 54
Courtney, David, 247
Cowens, Dave, 141, 203
Cox, David, 111
Crawford, Willie, 211
Crocker, Betty, 43
Crockett, Ivory, 191
Cruz, Joaquim, 54
Csonka, Joseph, 69
Csonka, Larry, 69, 75, 256
Cummings, Terry, 55
Curry, Bill, 18
Cutchin, Phil, 99

Dailey, Dr. Martel, 153
Dale, Jerry, 187
Dalton, Harry, 122
Damon, Lyle, 21
Danforth, Roy, 75
Dantley, Adrian, 163
Dark, Alvin, 190–91, 263
Darling, Ron, 38, 233
Dasbach, Kurt, 19
Daugherty, Duffy, 250
Davidson, Big Ben, 182
Davis, Kermit, 44
Davis, Lee, 216
Davis, Ron, 162
Dawkins, Darryl, 47, 50, 64,
    177, 194
Dawson, Andre, 267
Dean, Dizzy, 115
DeLamielleure, Joe, 147

273

Froemming, Bruce, 201
Fry, Hayden, 57
Fryzel, Dennis, 60
Ftorek, Robbie, 131

Gaines, Clark, 86
Gale, Rich, 33
Ganijan, Andy, 257
Gantner, Jim, 106
Garcia, Dave, 37
Gardner, Billy, 24, 51, 135, 154
Garland, Wayne, 145
Garner, Phil, 230
Garretson, Darell, 64
Garrison, Walt, 98
Garvey, Ed, 244
Garvey, Steve, 80, 120
Gavett, Peter, 31
Geronimo, Cesar, 121, 226
Giamatti, A. Bartlett, 36
Giannoulas, Ted, 93, 148
Gibron, Abe, 100
Gibson, Bob, 226
Gibson, Kirk, 91, 92
Gilbert, Rod, 80
Gillen, Pete, 46
Gillman, Sid, 5
Gmeinweiser, Bob. *See* Miller, Bob
Gminski, Mike, 17
Goalby, Bob, 18
Goldrick, Jim, 189
Gomez, Lefty, 185
Gomez, Preston, 7
Gonzales, Daniel, 8
Gonzalez, Luis, 253
Goux, Marv, 157
Govan, George, 160

Gowdy, Curt, 220
Grabarkewitz, Bill, 108, 228, 229
Graham, Billy, 263
Graham, Lou, 261
Grant, Bud, 244
Grant, Greg, 157
Green, Cornell, 141
Green, Dave, 207
Green, Mike, 149
Greene, Charlie, 49
Greene, Cornelius, 250, 262
Greeson, Stan, 67
Gregg, Forrest, 94
Grieve, Tom, 146
Griffey, Ken, 183
Griffin, Archie, 44
Grimm, Russ, 214
Gross, Greg, 231
Groza, Lou "The Toe," 20
Guerrero, Pedro, 175, 246
Guidry, Ron, 183
Guy, Tony, 16

Hadl, John, 157
Halas, George, 141, 150
Hall, Mel, 232
Hallacy, Pat, 49
Haller, Bill, 141
Haller, Tom, 141
Hannum, Alex, 179
Hansen, Glenn, 123
Hanson, Terry, 247
Hanzlik, Bill, 16
Hargrove, Mike, 33
Harper, Charlie, 70
Harper, Terry, 123
Harrell, Willard, 225
Harris, Del, 20

Harrison, Dennis, 42
Harshman, Marv, 181
Hartman, Jack, 57
Hatcher, Mickey, 26, 91
Havlicek, John, 110
Hawkins, Alex, 82
Hawkins, Burt, 162
Hayes, Elvin, 177
Hayes, Ken, 54
Hayes, Woody, 36, 67, 118,
    251, 262
Haynie, Barrie, 14
Heathcote, Jud, 102
Hebner, Richie, 49
Heiden, Beth, 176
Heinsohn, Tom, 213
Henderson, Dave, 26
Henderson, Steve, 26
Henry, Bunky, 192
Herndon, Larry, 267
Herzog, Whitey, 39, 210
Hilgenberg, Wally, 258
Hillman, Darnell, 171
Hiss, Arlene, 184
Hixson, Chuck, 184
Hogan, Don, 48
Holmes, Larry, 150
Holtz, Lou, 2, 4, 36, 45, 88,
    98, 105, 156, 237
Holtzman, Ken, 145
Hood, Jeff, 51
Horner, Bob, 146, 195
Horton, Ricky, 224
Houk, Ralph, 95, 238
Howard, Frank (baseball),
    75, 174
Howard, Frank (Clemson), 39
Howe, Gordie, 104, 186, 188,
    190

Howell, Jim, 142
Howser, Dick, 148
Hrabosky, Al, 36, 194
Hughes, Alfredrick, 24
Hunt, Lamar, 66
Hunter, Catfish, 214
Hurst, Bruce, 46

Irvin, LeRoy, 108

Jackson, Bo, 14, 18, 130
Jackson, Keith, 196
Jackson, Reggie, 23, 228
Jacobs, Joe, 54
James, Aaron, 146
James, Don, 142
Jenkins, Ferguson, 114
Jenner, Bruce, 158
Jobe, Ben, 46
John, Tommy, 201, 224
Johnson, Bob, 173
Johnson, Erza, 28
Johnson, Mike, 244
Johnson, Phil, 89
Jones, Dante, 211
Jones, Dwight, 208
Jones, Ed "Too Tall," 242
Jones, Larry, 57
Jones, Randy, 179
Jones, Victor, 24
Jordan, Buford, 145
Jurgensen, Sonny, 174, 176

Kaat, Jim, 7, 218, 222
Kamstra, Garry, 119
Kapp, Joe, 59, 138
Karras, Alex, 118, 151, 167
Kasten, Stan, 162
Kauffman, Bob, 95

Kauffman, Ewing, 99
Kelcher, Louie, 183
Kelleher, Mick, 232
Kelley, Rich, 148
Kelly, Tom, 32
Kelly, Vic, 111
Kemp, Jack, 136
Kerfeld, Charlie, 176
Kern, Jim, 212
Kerr, Johnny, 140, 179
Kiner, Ralph, 215
Kingman, Dave, 107
Kissing Bandit. *See* Roberts, Morganna
Kite, Greg, 168
Kittle, Ron, 15
Kleine, Joe, 163
Knight, Bobby, 60, 62, 102, 104
Knodel, Don, 48
Knotts, Doug, 42
Knox, Chuck, 61
Koufax, Sandy, 261
Kramer, Tommy, 120
Kranepool, Ed, 145
Kremser, Karl, 119
Kriek, Johan, 6, 86, 94
Krzyzewski, Mike, 104
Kuechenberg, Bob, 116
Kuehn, Harvey, 58
Kuhn, Bowie, 37, 114, 132, 220
Kunze, Dana, 211
Kush, Frank, 20, 240, 258

Lacewell, Larry, 100, 110
LaCoss, Mike, 74
LaLanne, Jack, 11
Lamb, Mike, 157

Lambert, Jack, 76
Lamont, Gene, 137
LaMotta, Jake, 93
Lamp, Dennis, 72
Landes, Stan, 61
Landry, Tom, 98, 174
Lane, Frank "Trader," 162
Langford, Rick, 231
LaPoint, Dave, 184, 223
LaRussa, Tony, 35
Lasorda, Tommy, 23, 25
Laver, Rod, 73, 143
Layden, Frank, 35, 173, 175
Layne, Bobby, 217
LeBaron, Eddie, 180, 237
Lee, Bill "Spaceman," 124, 193, 203, 251, 255
Lema, Tony, 257
Lemon, Jim, 210
Lemons, Abe, 111, 11, 14, 28, 58, 90, 97, 196, 239
Lenard, Darryl, 181
Lendl, Ivan, 255
Leonard, Debbie, 180
Leonard, Sugar Ray, 8
Lesuk, Bill, 80
Lewis, Bill, 84
Lincoln, Keith, 208
Lloyd, John, 191
Locke, Tates, 212
Lollar, Tim, 257
Lomax, Neil, 68
Lombardi, Vince, 20, 40
Lopes, Davey, 229
Lou, Yun, 131
Louie, Mareen "Peanut," 115
Louis, Joe, 149
Lourie, Michel, 217

Lovat, Tom, 180
Lowenstein, John, 32, 188
Lucas, Bill, 164
Lucas, Maurice, 114, 218
Luciano, Ron, 186, 198, 201
Lundquist, Steve, 175
Luro, Horatio, 93
Lutz, Bob, 53

Mack, Tom, 253
Madden, John, 215, 238, 246
Mallory, Bill, 56
Malone, Moses, 62
Maltbie, Roger, 17
Mandarich, Tony, 71
Manning, Danny, 158
Manson, Charles, 48
Mantle, Mickey, 83, 209
Manumaleuma, Frank, 111
Mara, Wellington, 164
Maranville, Rabbit, 81
Marsh, Bill, 237
Marshall, Mike, 268
Martin, Ben, 235, 253
Martin, Billy, 78, 81, 111, 187, 209
Martin, Donnie, 208
Martin, James "The Bull," 113
Martin, John, 221
Martin, Lynn, 90
Martin, Slater, 17
Martinez, Carmelo, 14
Martinez, Teddy, 13
Martzoff, Ron, 11
Mason, Roger, 267
Matuszak, John, 27
Mauch, Gene, 26, 76, 237
Mays, Willie, 228

McAdoo, Bob, 179, 211
McBride, Bake, 212
McCarthy, John, 51
McCloskey, Jack, 165, 262
McDaniel, Xavier, 80
McDonagh, Matt, 180
McGee, Max, 40
McGlothlin, Jim, 5
McGraw, Tug, 163
McGuire, Al, 21, 77, 118, 136
McGuire, Frank, 29
McGwire, Mark, 82
McHone, Phil, 23
McKay, Jim, 109
McKay, John, 72, 113, 167, 254, 268
McKeon, Jack, 194, 250
McLean, Ron, 212
McMahon, Jack, 134
McMahon, Jim, 117
McNall, Bruce, 131
McVay, John, 164
McWilliams, David, 168
Medich, Doc, 148
Meek, Dick, 49
Menne, Bob, 249
Meriwether, Dr. Delano, 166
Merril, Casey, 145
Metcalf, Shelby, 117
Metzger, Roger, 263
Michael, Gene, 74
Michaels, Al, 249
Mihalak, Paul, 168
Miller, Bob, 111
Miller, Johnny, 26, 188
Millo, Paul, 36
Mills, Chuck, 42, 45
Minnifield, Frank, 168

Mitchell, Aaron, 114
Mitchell, Jack, 157
Mix, Ron, 10
Montoya, Max, 147
Mooney, Frank, 3
Moore, Archie, 108, 215
Moore, Butch, 113
Morris, Sam, 149
Morrison, Jim, 223
Morrison, Stan, 30, 88
Moses, Edwin, 58
Motta, Dick, 71
Mueller, Tom, 21
Muncie, Chuck, 166
Murcer, Bobby, 44
Murphy, Bob, 78
Murphy, Ed, 90
Murphy, Gene, 85

Nagurski, Bronco, 210
Namath, Joe, 5, 182, 206
Nastase, Ilie, 78, 94
Navratilova, Martina, 71, 187
Neale, Harry, 238
Neary, Bill, 118
Neely, Jess, 55
Neil, Randy, 91
Nelford, Jim, 250
Nelson, Lindsey, 24, 121
Nevitt, Chuck, 73
Newcombe, John, 9
Newlin, Mike, 56
Newton, C. M., 56, 234
Nichols, Bobby, 87
Nicklaus, Jack, 84, 125, 193, 200
Nolan, Dick, 139
Noll, Chuck, 137

Norton, Ken, 23, 84
Nye, Blaine, 2

O'Brien, Patrick, 248
O'Brien, Syd, 217
Odom, Steve, 195
Ogden, Bud, 168
Olajuwon, Akeem, 178
Oldfield, Brian, 36, 151
Oleynick, Frank, 149
Olivares, Ruben, 217
Oliver, Gene, 261
Ontiveros, Steve, 196
Orr, Johnny, 61
Owens, Jesse, 218
Ownby, Rick, 222
Ozark, Danny, 106, 108, 187, 222, 238

Paciorek, Tom, 135
Palmer, Arnold, 29, 96
Parcells, Bill, 209
Pardee, Jack, 259
Parish, Robert, 235
Parker, Dave, 72
Parker, Harry, 222
Parker, Wes, 61
Parseghian, Ara, 239
Pastorini, Dan, 250
Patek, Freddie, 181
Paterno, Joe, 266
Patterson, Floyd, 167
Paul, Gabe, 2
Payton, Walter, 150, 242
Pearson, Preston, 74
Pell, Charley, 108-9
Penders, Tom, 190
Penske, Roger, 251
Pep, Willie, 10, 95

Walseth, Russell "Sox," 90
Walton, Bill, 108
Warfield, Paul, 208
Warmath, Murray, 167
Washington, Claudell, 66, 117
Waters, Buck, 158
Waters, Charlie, 18, 114
Wathan, John, 189
Watson, Bob, 76
Watson, Glenn, 183
Watson, Tom, 85, 256
Weaver, Earl, 63
Welch, Bob, 228
Welles, Terry, 92
Wells, Lanky, 156
Weltlich, Bob, 57
Wepner, Chuck, 123, 179
West, Jerry, 146
White, Bill, 127
White, Dave, 265
White, Vanna, 17
Wilhelm, Hoyt, 97
Wilkens, Jeff, 35
Wilkens, Lenny, 16
Williams, Buck, 170
Williams, Dick, 25, 36, 257

Williams, Gary, 40
Williams, Mark, 236
Williams, Steve, 183, 256
Willis, Kevin, 80
Wills, Maury, 61, 75
Wilson, Steve, 28
Wilson, Willie, 128
Winfield, Dave, 143
Winfield, Jim, 254
Winslow, Kellen, 191
Wohlford, Jim, 87
Wolf, David, 242
Worthen, Sam, 4
Wyche, Sam, 57
Wynn, Early, 225

Yamin, Joe, 250
Yastrzemski, Carl, 124
Yeager, Steve, 10, 92
Yeoman, Bill, 4
Yepremian, Garo, 194

Zarley, Kermit, 110
Zimmer, Don, 114
Zimmer, Tom, 131
Zorn, Jim, 251